An Ocean of Blessings

An Ocean of Blessings

Heart Teachings of Drubwang Penor Rinpoche

TRANSLATED BY
Ani Jinba Palmo

EDITED BY
Michael Tweed

FOREWORDS BY
Dzongsar Khyentse Rinpoche
Sogyal Rinpoche
Mugsang Kuchen Rinpoche
Khenchen Tsewang Gyatso

SNOW LION
BOULDER
2017

Snow Lion
An imprint of Shambhala Publications, Inc.
4720 Walnut Street
Boulder, Colorado 80301
www.shambhala.com

© 2017 by Palyul Ling International
Foreword by Sogyal Rinpoche © 2017 by Tertön Sogyal Trust

Frontispiece: Drubwang Penor Rinpoche, empowerment at
Palyul Retreat Center, upstate New York (Photo © 2006 by Mannie Garcia).

9 8 7 6 5 4 3 2 1

First Edition
Printed in the United States of America

⊚ This edition is printed on acid-free paper that meets
the American National Standards Institute Z39.48 Standard.
♻ This book is printed on 30% postconsumer recycled paper.
For more information please visit www.shambhala.com.

Distributed in the United States by Penguin Random House LLC
and in Canada by Random House of Canada Ltd

LIBRARY OF CONGRESS CATALOGING-IN-PUBLICATION DATA
Names: Penor Rinpoche III, 1932–2009, author. | Tweed, Michael, editor.
Title: An ocean of blessings: heart teachings of Drubwang Penor Rinpoche /
    Penor Rinpoche; translated by Ani Jinba; edited by Michael Tweed.
Description: First edition. | Boulder: Snow Lion, 2017. | Translated from Tibetan.
Identifiers: LCCN 2016056893 | ISBN 9781559394697 (pbk.: acid-free paper)
Subjects: LCSH: Penor Rinpoche III, 1932–2009—Teachings. | Buddhism.
Classification: LCC BQ978.E46 P46 2017 | DDC 294.3/420423—dc23
LC record available at https://lccn.loc.gov/2016056893

Contents

Foreword

Dzongsar Khyentse Rinpoche

The Tibetan word *jin-lap* is loosely translated as "blessings." Jin-lap transforms our whole being—our body, our speech, the way we think, how we understand phenomena, and the way we relate to ourselves and the world. Ultimately, however, what jin-lap does is to break the shell of our ego and force us to see the true nature of our minds.

Among many other causes and conditions, in the Vajrayana it is the guru who is considered the most important and indeed supreme cause for doing all the above. In fact, that force and power is all the stronger if the guru is a realized being, if he is genuinely compassionate, and if he considers helping sentient beings the main purpose of his existence.

Kyabje Penor Rinpoche is one such great master of our time, as unanimously confirmed time and again by some of the most illustrious masters of the past hundred years, including Kyabje Dudjom Rinpoche, Kyabje Dilgo Khyentse Rinpoche, and Khenpo Jigme Phuntsok. I don't have to detail Penor Rinpoche's perseverance and dedication in tirelessly propagating the Dharma to benefit sentient beings. That is all there to be seen in his actions and in his continuing legacy.

Here is a very precious collection of Kyabje Penor Rinpoche's teachings. I have no doubt that these teachings, if not a blessing in themselves, will be a bridge to receive jin-lap from the master himself. Ani Jinba Palmo's long association with and marination in the Buddhadharma have certainly helped her to closely translate and interpret the words of this great master. These teachings should not be kept on a bookshelf but read, and not only read but put into practice.

Bodhgaya, November 2016

FOREWORD

SOGYAL RINPOCHE

IT IS A great blessing and honor to be invited to introduce this anthology of teachings by His Holiness Penor Rinpoche, who was not only one of the most important Tibetan Buddhist masters of the twentieth century, but also a visionary and a leader who played a vital and timely role in keeping alive the profound teachings and practices of the Buddhist tradition of Tibet.

Looking back now, we all remember only too readily how the twentieth century witnessed a long period of turmoil, misery, and upheaval in Tibet. It was a time when the sheer survival of the Tibetan people and their unique Buddhist culture seemed in doubt. I will never forget how in the spring of 1959 I was in Sikkim, a Himalayan kingdom and one of the hidden lands of Guru Padmasambhava, alongside my master Jamyang Khyentse Chökyi Lodrö, whose health was gradually failing. Later, when summer came, he passed away. During those few months of mounting uncertainty, pieces of bleak and terrible news about the tragic events in Tibet trickled through, day by day. At the same time, thousands upon thousands of ordinary Tibetan men, women, and children, as well as monks, nuns, and lamas, were making the long and dangerous journey from their homeland across the Himalayas into exile. Among them were a number of great Buddhist masters, and one of them was Kyabje Penor Rinpoche.

Years later, we would all hear of how Penor Rinpoche, the head of the great monastery of Palyul in eastern Tibet—one of the six "mother" monasteries in the Ngagyur Nyingma tradition—had eventually found himself in Mysore in southern India with a few monks and a mere 300 rupees to his name. Yet with his incredible vision, ingenuity, and determination, and by throwing himself into hard manual labor—digging, building, driving, as well as buying and fetching supplies—he had gradually brought into existence what was to become one of the largest Tibetan monasteries in exile. The Namdroling monastery complex he founded is now home to thousands of monks and nuns. Penor Rinpoche is someone who will go down in history as one of the prime architects in the spread of Tibetan Buddhism, and especially of the Ngagyur Nyingma tradition.

Penor Rinpoche was universally respected on account of the meticulous care he took—whether it was in passing on all the most important empowerments and transmissions; preserving the authenticity of the tradition along with its rare texts; training the Palyul lineage holders and lamas, for example, the three "heart sons" Karma Kuchen Rinpoche, Khentrul Gyangkhang Rinpoche, and Mugsang Kuchen Rinpoche; or ordaining countless monks and nuns. Again and again, he would invite the great Tibetan masters to pass on teachings to the young tulkus and lamas. Kyabje Dilgo Khyentse Rinpoche, for example, whom Penor Rinpoche saw as Vajradhara, the primordial buddha in person, visited Namdroling on numerous occasions and granted many transmissions.

Overcoming enormous difficulties and against all odds, Penor Rinpoche succeeded in bringing together outstanding scholars from all traditions—I think of Khenpo Rinchen from the Sakya tradition, for example—to establish a shedra, or college of advanced Buddhist studies, that has set new standards of excellence in scholarship for the Ngagyur Nyingma tradition. This was a truly historic achievement, for today Namdroling is famous for its world-class Ngagyur Nyingma University, which is led by outstanding authorities such as Khenchen Pema Sherab, Khenchen Namdrol, and Khenchen Tsewang Gyatso, and has sent khenpos and teachers to Nyingma monasteries and Dharma communities in many parts of the world, especially to the Himalayan regions like Bhutan and Nepal. To sum up, Penor Rinpoche was truly what you might call a "hands-on lama" who, during a very challenging time for Tibetan people, single-handedly pieced together the entire community around Namdroling. He not only cared for the monks and nuns, but equally for the lay community by founding schools and hospitals, which were all part of the scope of his vast compassionate vision.

Penor Rinpoche was an exceptional leader who personally galvanized and brought together the sometimes scattered Nyingma tradition. He and his monks oversaw much of the organization of the Nyingma Monlam Chenmo, the great annual prayer festival held at Bodhgaya, and under his leadership it grew stronger and stronger. Returning to Tibet on four occasions, Penor Rinpoche rebuilt and renovated monasteries, including the main Palyul monastery in Kham and many of its branch monasteries; gave empowerments, transmissions, and teachings to thousands; and ordained many monks and nuns. No wonder that in 1993, following in the footsteps of Kyabje Dudjom Rinpoche and Kyabje Dilgo Khyentse Rinpoche, he was chosen by the Nyingma community as the supreme head of the Nyingma order, a responsibility he passed on to His Holiness Mindrolling Trichen Rinpoche in 2001.

Penor Rinpoche visited countries all over the world, and first traveled to the West in the 1980s. In 1988, I invited him to London where he gave the complete empowerments of "The Four Parts of the Nyingtik" (*Nyingtik Yabshi*), which are crucial for the practice of the Great Perfection (Dzogchen), along with a number of other important initiations. In 1995, during a lengthy tour of the West, Rinpoche spent a whole month in Europe at our invitation. He first taught in Paris and London, and then at the end of July, he spent ten days in Lerab Ling, Rigpa's retreat center near Montpellier in southern France. Once again, he granted the *Nyingtik Yabshi* empowerments, this time to six hundred students. He led a Vajrakilaya *dokpa*, a practice for averting misfortune and inauspicious circumstances, from the *terma* revelation of Ratna Lingpa, and conferred the long bodhisattva vow according to the approach of Nagarjuna, commenting that it was only the third time in his life that he had done so.

All through that year, when Penor Rinpoche was touring North America and Europe, I noticed that wherever he traveled, he did everything within his power to encourage and strengthen the different groups and communities practicing the Nyingma teachings, and in particular to bring them together in a spirit of harmony. To take the example of our own community, because he saw what we were seeking to achieve, he always held Rigpa in his wisdom mind with tremendous compassion, and I know he gave the same care to every other center and organization. At every turn, Penor Rinpoche was there to guide and inspire us with his spiritual support. Among the many things we have to thank him for, he kindly gave his blessing to the Rigpa Shedra's branch in Nepal, where classes are held each year under the direction of Khenchen Namdrol.

Although I always knew Penor Rinpoche to be one of our greatest living lamas, it was only when my beloved master, Nyoshul Khenpo Jamyang Dorje, brought me closer to him that I began to discover just how extraordinary he was. Nyoshul Khen Rinpoche, one of the foremost exponents of the Dzogchen teachings, had spent a long time at Namdroling. In fact, he had played a large and formative part in the development of the monastery and was adored by the whole community, especially by Penor Rinpoche.

I had often heard Nyoshul Khenpo talk about the great Khenpo Ngakchung, a key figure in the transmission of the lineage of the Dzogchen pith instructions. Khenpo Ngakchung had been among the principal disciples of Nyoshul Lungtok Tenpe Nyima, who was the student of Patrul Rinpoche and the heir to his Dzogchen lineage. It was Khenpo Ngakchung who recognized his master Nyoshul Lungtok's incarnation, Lungtrul Shedrup Tenpe Nyima. And years later, he also recognized Penor Rinpoche as the incarnation of the Second Drubwang Pema Norbu.

True to the tradition, Penor Rinpoche would invariably emphasize in his teachings the importance of guru yoga, devotion, and the blessing of the master for a person to realize the pure awareness of the nature of mind. As he points out in this book, "there are many practitioners who have realized the nature of mind and attained perfect enlightenment *just by* doing guru yoga." At Lerab Ling, I remember the tears of devotion streaming down his face when, in expressing our deep respect for him, we compared him to Dilgo Khyentse Rinpoche and the great masters of the past. With his characteristic humility, he replied by likening himself to a dog, who takes over once the humans have left. Again and again, Penor Rinpoche would point out how essential it is to follow a master over a considerable period of time, to let go of doubt and uncertainty, and to see all hardships and difficulties, whatever they may be, as part of the path. As he explains in these pages, "by following one's master with such strong and unwavering devotion the result can really be quite extraordinary."

I was fascinated when one day he recounted the story of how his master Lungtrul Shedrup Tenpe Nyima had been brought up by Khenpo Ngakchung. Khenpo kept Lungtrul, who was the incarnation of his own teacher Nyoshul Lungtok, in his residence and made him sweep the floor, prepare his food, and work in the kitchen. While he was still young, he would be sent to the grasslands to take care of the cattle. However, whenever Khenpo Ngakchung gave transmissions or empowerments, he made sure Lungtrul was present, although he assigned him the humblest seat, right by the door. At the same time, he would never encourage or allow him to do any studies. Visiting lamas were concerned and pressed Khenpo to make the young incarnation study and begin his training in earnest, but still Khenpo

Ngakchung waited. When he saw that he was ready and that his basic being had been transformed, he gave him the entire training, especially in the great oral lineage of pith instructions, after which Lungtrul became an extraordinary master, unlike any other. He was Khenpo Ngakchung's most cherished heart son and the holder of "the ultimate lineage of realization."

Lungtrul Shedrup Tenpe Nyima was one of Penor Rinpoche's most important root teachers, the one who gave him the mind-to-mind transmission of the Dzogchen teachings. He was also Nyoshul Khenpo's root lama. In his history of the Dzogchen lineage masters, Nyoshul Khenpo quotes Penor Rinpoche's own words:

> When I requested Lungtok Choktrul for the oral transmission of the pith instructions, such as the root volumes of the *Longchen Nyingtik* and the *Yeshe Lama*, he granted me the direct introduction to these teachings twice, going through them section by section. The second occasion was like the sun rising at the break of day. From that moment on, I found that my realization was not subject to any transition or change. It seemed that this was the experience of primordial wisdom, the unity of awareness and emptiness, in all its nakedness.

Penor Rinpoche was clearly a Dzogchen master whose realization was extraordinary. Dilgo Khyentse Rinpoche said of him: "Penor Rinpoche is a saint who has transcended the boundaries of the ordinary world." Interestingly, Penor Rinpoche told Nyoshul Khenpo that, rather than during formal meditation sessions, it was in everyday life and in action that he found his realization was enhanced and became even more vibrant.

At the same time, Penor Rinpoche was a very powerful Vajrayana master. Once he confided to me that he had a special connection with Vajrakilaya, the enlightened activity of all the buddhas, so much so that when he was young, if he recited a few thousand mantras of Vajrakilaya and blew upon a ritual implement like a sword, it would instantly emit a crackling sound and give off sparks and jets of flame. In fact, there are many such accounts of Penor Rinpoche's great realization and extraordinary powers. I heard that Khenchen Jigme Phuntsok Rinpoche said he believed Penor Rinpoche was an enlightened buddha living among us.

It was therefore thanks to Nyoshul Khenpo that I enjoyed a close and deepening link with this great master, and I was fortunate to spend time with him on a number of occasions when he would speak about his own practice, intimate moments when he revealed his greatness, even though he was extraordinarily humble. Once, in the year 2000, when His Holiness the Dalai Lama was visiting the Dzogchen monastery in southern India, Penor Rinpoche was invited as well. Quite unexpectedly, I spent a number of days with him and was struck by the depth of his knowledge, wisdom, kindness, integrity, and strength of character. We speak of the guru as being replete or weighty with precious qualities like these, and in the case of Penor Rinpoche this was self-evident, as they were all embodied in his very presence.

In fact, it was merely through his presence that things were accomplished. I was constantly amazed by how, whatever the obstacles to any given undertaking and however unlikely the outcome, he would remain unruffled, and in the most uncanny ways he always seemed to manage to meet his goals. Funds would somehow appear, things would effortlessly fall into place, and a given project would come into being. As I spent more time with Penor Rinpoche, my respect for him grew more and more profound. Whenever I think of him now, it is that sense of his presence that returns to me, that unwavering confidence and immovable composure that made us realize that he was never separate from the state of dharmakaya.

In this rare collection of his teachings translated into English, Penor Rinpoche defines very clearly the indispensable qualities and principles of the Dharma and how to integrate them into our lives. Here you will find vital teachings for life and death, sprinkled with lively anecdotes, all of which somehow capture Rinpoche's directness and compassion, as well as his deep humility. As we can read in these pages, Penor Rinpoche would always stress the importance of stability for a practitioner, and I vividly recall a remarkable teaching he gave at our center in London, during which he insisted on three additional qualities:

> The most important things, as I say again and again, are faith, heartfelt devotion, and pure perception. These three are the most essential points, the most important qualities we need while on the path. You need to know that their whole purpose is not for the lama's sake, nor for the teaching, but for your sake, for the sake of your own development. We should have a mind that is stable, that will not waver and change, and that is free from hesitation and doubt.

Penor Rinpoche was a unique master, and his influence, I feel, will endure and reverberate for centuries to come. He paved the way for a new era of Tibetan Buddhism as it took root all over the world, and this he did with the foresight and sense of purpose that set him apart from other masters. As each year goes by, I think we will realize more and more the immense scale and far-reaching impact of his legacy. After he passed away in 2009, for a brief period I felt concerned about the future of Namdroling, and yet all my worries evaporated when I witnessed how the tulkus, the khenpos, and the whole monastic community continued to implement his vision even more dynamically than before.

How fortunate we all are, followers of Tibetan Buddhism and especially the Ngagyur Nyingma tradition, that Penor Rinpoche appeared among us at such a critical moment. His whole life was offered in the service of the teachings, so they would survive, and in the service of beings everywhere. He left the Nyingma tradition stronger and more unified perhaps than at any time in its history. We owe him so much. How blessed we are too, to have any connection to this great being, through having seen him, hearing his instructions, or reading his teachings in books such as this one. How wonderful it is that Penor Rinpoche's incarnation has been found and enthroned at the great Palyul monastery in Tibet. May he grow to be as glorious a manifestation as Penor Rinpoche himself, and may Penor Rinpoche's vision and work flourish and continue long into the future.

Finally, we should be forever grateful to Ani Jinba Palmo for rendering into English these precious teachings from such an extraordinary master and spiritual leader. May they be a source of enduring inspiration, knowledge, and awareness to all who read them, filling all readers with blessings, courage, and certainty, and energizing them on their path toward enlightenment.

Lerabling, September 2016

FOREWORD

MUGSANG KUCHEN RINPOCHE

KYABJE PENOR RINPOCHE'S vision, courage, and efforts for the sake of sentient beings and the Buddha's teachings are well known, so here I would like to share some of his seemingly ordinary activities that are actually quite extraordinary, which I have witnessed with my own eyes. I would like to share such stories because I think that when a great lama like Kyabje Penor Rinpoche behaves like an ordinary person, his example is an important lesson for us all.

Rinpoche had a multifaceted personality that would be difficult to find these days. He was not only a lama who sat on the throne and gave teachings, empowerments, reading transmissions, and so forth; he was also a father, a mother, a teacher, a doctor, a nurse, a healer, and even a cook and caretaker. When I reflect on his actions, I find that they set him apart from others. He was very special, even when compared to other great lamas.

In the early days after he arrived in India, he did not have much money. Nonetheless, putting forth great effort, often carrying the bricks himself, he laid a foundation and built a large temple with the limited resources he had. This was Namdroling's first temple where the congregation of monks would perform Buddhist ceremonies and conduct teachings.

Far away from the temple, he built a monastery kitchen, and on the opposite side, equally far away, he constructed a small temple that housed a big prayer wheel. To ordinary eyes, it seemed strange and awkward to have built these three lone structures so distant from one another. Many of Rinpoche's students couldn't understand why he had done so and questioned his plans, but Rinpoche just carried on, undisturbed by what others thought.

Over time, Namdroling expanded as numerous temples, classrooms, dormitories, and stupas were constructed. When you look at the layout of the monastery today, you can understand how farsighted Rinpoche's vision was, as those three original structures now form the heart and the boundaries of Namdroling.

When I was just two years of age, Rinpoche recognized me as the reincarnation of Mugsang Kuchen. He brought me to the monastery and took care of me even better than my loving parents.

In those early days, even though Rinpoche wouldn't go to bed until eleven p.m., he would still get up each morning at three o'clock. Upon arising he would prepare the shrine offerings, do a hundred prostrations, and engage in his practice. After that, around six thirty a.m., he would make breakfast for everyone and then wake up all the tulkus and attendants. Assuming the role of our mother, he would help me and the other little ones wash and put on our robes. Once we were ready, we would all eat breakfast together. Then it would be time for him to go to the refugee camps to perform religious services. The attendants had to prepare lunch and dinner and also clean the water offering bowls after throwing out the water. If they failed to perform any of these responsibilities, they would get a scolding from Rinpoche.

In the evening, before we went to sleep, Rinpoche would read us stories from the biographies of the great masters of the past, especially biographies of the Palyul throne holders, as well as accounts of the outer, inner, and secret aspects of the main Palyul monastery.

Every week Rinpoche himself would drive to Mysore in the hot sun to buy vegetables and other supplies. Often he would also bring back toys and sweets for the young tulkus and monks.

During the summer, we would often go to Deer Park River for a swim. Whenever a monk, usually a young one, was in danger of drowning, Rinpoche would dive into the river and save the monk himself. However, as the monastery expanded, these outings grew as well, so he would always advise everyone to be very careful when they went swimming. Unfortunately, a number of our monks still ended up drowning, so Rinpoche constructed sixteen stupas on the northern side of the monastery to avert harm from the river; as a result, the number of deaths fell drastically.

When I was about seven or eight years old, Penor Rinpoche had become so busy that, together with the other young tulkus Kyabje Karma Kuchen and Khentrul Gyangkhang Rinpoche, I was assigned to Lama Sonam Tenzin to continue my training in reading and writing. When we had grown up a bit more, we went to study at the shedra, the scriptural college. From Rinpoche himself, as well as from many other masters he had invited, such as Kyabje Dilgo Khyentse, we received the empowerments, transmissions, and instructions of the Kama and Terma of the Early Translation school. In fact, after escaping Tibet, Kyabje Penor Rinpoche was the first master in India to spread the instructions, empowerments, and oral transmissions of the *Sutra That Gathers All Intentions*. When I think about all this now, I am awed by how immeasurable his kindness actually was.

Later, when I had grown up, he often gave me sound practical advice, for example, "On the one hand, there will be hundreds of people who will praise you, yet on the other hand, there will be a thousand who will despise you. So do not lose focus; always carry out your responsibilities without fail."

One of Rinpoche's many qualities was his accessibility to the public. People from the eighteen camps of the Bylakuppe Tibetan settlement—high and low, rich and poor, learned and uneducated—would come to see him with all kinds of problems, and Rinpoche would always be there to attend to their needs. Even late at night people would come to request prayers for those who had fallen ill or died. Rinpoche always readily fulfilled their wishes and spent considerable time praying for both the living and the dead.

Just as Lord Buddha nursed his disciples who were ill and bedridden, Rinpoche was a doctor and a nurse to any of his monks who got sick or injured. Monks would come to him with all types of illnesses—headaches, stomachaches, broken bones, sores, bruises, and so forth. Rinpoche would give them Tibetan medicinal pills and some mendrup that he had prepared from herbs and ground-up precious stones and blessed during special great accomplishment rituals. He would recite mantras and blow on the affected area or do a mo divination and give advice to those who needed more intensive care or treatment at a nearby hospital. In short, he perfectly undertook the compassionate role of a healer.

The majority of the local people of Bylakuppe are farmers whose livelihood depends on rain. Whenever there was a drought, at the request of the public, Rinpoche would perform rain rituals to moisten the soil and improve the crops. Thus, he became known locally as "the rain lama." From time to time he would also assemble a variety of precious vases, consecrated through proper Secret Mantra rituals and filled with gems and other priceless materials: vases for enhancing soil fertility, naga vases, wealth vases, and so on, often thousands at a time. He would then freely distribute these vases to whoever needed them.

One day around 2001, Rinpoche asked me to gather a few monks to cut down the lush green juniper trees growing on and around the monastery's central lawn. So I requested the treasurer to send some of the monks who were working under him.

Rinpoche was present as the monks began chopping down the trees one by one. It was sad to see those beautiful trees cut down, as they were still very much alive and provided shelter from the sun for residents and visitors alike. While they were being chopped down, local Tibetans who knew Rinpoche pleaded with him, "Rinpoche, please don't cut down the trees! They are not so old, and they provide us with shade." Rinpoche replied, "Be quiet! You don't know why I'm doing this." And he proceeded as planned.

After the trees were felled, his true purpose became apparent as around forty frogs of different sizes that had been trapped in the tree trunks were released from their prison. They were the kind of beings referred to in the scriptures as inhabitants of the ephemeral hells. With his clairvoyance Rinpoche had seen them suffering inside the trees and knew that it was the right time to free them. He ordered the monks to collect the live frogs and release them in the river nearby.

Rinpoche's compassion truly knew no bounds, even when it came with great personal risk. He once told me that he was poisoned three times by a local Tibetan man. This was done under the pretext of offering him food. Rinpoche said that he could tell by the odor that the food contained poison. Nonetheless, each time he happily ate the poisoned food, returned to his residence, and took a handful of mendrup.

The third attempt occurred when Rinpoche was presiding over an accomplishment ceremony at the old Namdroling Temple, which is now the Zangdog Palri Temple. Penor Rinpoche said that he actually saw the perpetrator switch his bowl with one containing the poisoned food. After eating some, he got very sick and dizzy, to the point that he was unable to see anything in front of him. He left the ceremony without finishing it, returned to his residence, and, just as he had done the previous two times, took a handful of mendrup. Unfortunately, however, this time it didn't work, and he had to be taken to the hospital for detoxification. Even so, Rinpoche told me that he never gave rise to feelings of anger, revenge, or enmity toward the frustrated murderer. Instead, he showered the man with presents, and in no time, the wrongdoer's attitude and harmful tendencies were replaced with reverence for Rinpoche. After this, though, at the request of his attendants and students, during public ceremonies Rinpoche no longer ate food that had been not been prepared in the monastery.

These are just a few of the extraordinary stories in the life of Kyabje Penor Rinpoche, who truly was the embodiment of Vimalamitra and Guru Rinpoche. I rejoice that his teachings are now available not only to those who had the good fortune to have met him but also to those who did not, and that now anyone can receive his blessings by reading and studying the teachings in this precious book. May it be of great benefit to all!

Namdroling, January 2017

Foreword

KHENCHEN TSEWANG GYATSO

Great master Vimalamitra, master of all panditas,
Kindly manifesting in nirmanakaya form,
Renowned as Drubwang Pema Norbu,
I bow down to you with sincere devotion and faith.
Kindly bestow blessings through your compassion and great wisdom.
Dharmakaya guru, primordially pure,
Sambhogakaya guru, endowed with all enlightened qualities, and
Nirmanakaya guru, compassionately manifesting in human form,
I pay homage and prostrate at your lotus feet.
Kindly hold us in your presence and bestow your blessings and
    accomplishments.

I wish to write a few lines regarding our great guru, Kyabje Drubwang Pema
Norbu Rinpoche, well known to all of us as a buddha in human form: how
he was recognized as the reincarnation of the second Penor Rinpoche, his
miraculous Dharma activities, and how he benefited countless beings.

The fifth Dzogchen Rinpoche, Thubten Chödor, prophesied the circumstances of Drubwang Pema Norbu's birth, saying:

In the upper region of sacred Powo,
At the foot of a majestic hill,
Surrounded by beautiful trees and lakes,
With a large river flowing from the south,
To a couple bearing the names Sonam and Kyi,
A noble child will be born in the Water Monkey year.

Possessing great qualities,
He will benefit the teachings and many beings.

In accordance with this prophecy, the reincarnation of Drubwang Pema Norbu was found in the eastern Tibetan region of Kham. He was born in 1932, the Water Monkey year. The great master Khenpo Ngakchung also confirmed him to be the authentic reincarnation of the second Drubwang Penor Rinpoche.

In 1936, at the age of four, he was invited to the main Palyul monastery, where he first received refuge vows and a Manjushri empowerment from his master Khenpo Ngakchung, who also composed the long-life prayer for Penor Rinpoche that was chanted throughout his lifetime.

At the age of twelve, Penor Rinpoche was enthroned as the eleventh throne holder of the Palyul lineage by his spiritual master Thubten Chökyi Dawa and Karma Kuchen Rinpoche, the tenth throne holder.

Rinpoche received transmissions of all the major lineages from numerous qualified masters, including teachings on sutra and tantra, as well as empowerments of the four categories of tantra. Most of the teachings and instructions on the inner tantras and Dzogchen practice instructions were received from his root teacher, the previous Palyul Choktrul Rinpoche, and the fourth Karma Kuchen Rinpoche.

From childhood through to his teenage years, Rinpoche studied Buddhadharma and philosophy, including the sciences of medicine and astrology. Under his guru's guidance, he entered retreat to dedicate his time and effort to the preliminary practices known as *ngöndro*, the yogic exercises known as *tsalung*, as well as deity yoga and Dzogchen meditation. As a result of his practice, he gained complete mastery over all the instructions, displaying wonderful signs of realization and accomplishment, including weaving thread into blessing cords with his tongue, miraculously writing the letter *A* on conch shells, gluing a broken vajra back together using his own saliva, and throwing his teacup from the second story to the pavement without it breaking. There are many more instances of miraculous displays arising from the great accomplishments of his practice.

Later, after the upheaval in Tibet, Rinpoche left for India, arriving in the northeastern town of Balingpung. It was there that I met him for the first time, when I was just seven years old. Rinpoche blessed me and my family, placing his hand on our heads. The moment I received his blessing, I knew instantly and without any doubt that I was connected to him.

Unfortunately, our meeting was cut short since we did not have the required permit to remain in Balingpung.

After that, the Indian government kindly sent Rinpoche and other Tibetan refugees to a settlement in the Mysore district of south India. Rinpoche arrived there as a refugee in 1960. Like a great yogi, empty-handed and full of hope, Rinpoche had a vision of establishing a complete monastic institution that would provide the highest standard of training in all fields of Buddhism. He dedicated the rest of his life to the establishment of Namdroling Monastery, an institution to educate monks and nuns equally and serve the needs of the local Tibetan and Indian communities.

Without resources or expectations, Rinpoche worked tirelessly. With complete dedication, he spent everything he had and overcame many hardships in order to build his monastery. The noble institutions he established include Ngagyur Nyingma Institute (center for higher Buddhist studies and research), Tsogyal Shedrubling (Namdroling's nunnery), Samten Öseling (three-year retreat center), and Yeshe Ösel Sherab Raldriling (secondary school). His intention was always to benefit future generations by preserving the teachings and culture of the Dharma. He dedicated himself wholeheartedly to the welfare of all who wished to join the community.

I have heard and read about the activities of many bodhisattvas from scriptural sources, but my real-life experience of a bodhisattva comes from Rinpoche, who was undoubtedly an authentic example of a great bodhisattva in practice. There is no need to go into extensive detail regarding Rinpoche's immeasurable bodhisattva activities, for I know that many readers are fortunate enough to have experienced them directly in their own lives.

What I have related here is just one aspect of Rinpoche's outer activities and accomplishments as they have benefited the lives and communities of many Tibetans and local families. In fact, his compassionate activities reached inconceivably far and wide, advancing monastic training and education in every corner of the world. With his great wisdom and unconditional love, Rinpoche traveled all around the world to establish Dharma centers that would benefit all beings equally, regardless of their race or color or whether they were rich or poor.

His benevolent inner and secret activities to propagate Buddhism and its practices have benefited beings unimaginably, not only those in the Himalayan regions. The brilliant sunshine of Dharma radiating in all directions has dispelled the darkness of sentient beings and awakened them to the light of wisdom illuminating the four directions.

Please read with joy these heart instructions from our root master, whose enlightened qualities are equal to the Buddha's and whose kindness and care for us is even greater than that of the Buddha.

I sincerely appreciate all the work that went into translating and editing this valuable collection of teachings. Thanks to everyone who helped to bring this precious treasure of knowledge into existence in book form.

This book is the Buddhist GPS with navigation controls set for enlightenment, nirvana, and the end of suffering in samsara. Please be sure you do not recalculate your route! I am confident that these nectar-like instructions, if put into practice, will benefit all sentient beings and enable them to recognize their primordial pure nature.

With warm wishes, blessings, and love to you all.

New York, January 2017

Translator's Preface

A FEW YEARS AGO, several of Drubwang Pema Norbu Rinpoche's students asked me to translate some of his teachings in order to publish them as a book. These were teachings that Rinpoche gave during his annual seminars at the Palyul Retreat Center in upstate New York between 2000 and 2008. Before starting the main topic of the seminar, Rinpoche would always give an introductory talk about the importance of guru yoga, mingling one's mind with the master's mind, devotion, faith, pure perception, bodhichitta, and applying the practice in one's daily life; these then became the main topics of this book.

It was a great privilege and joy to take on this project, and after listening to 130 talks, I chose about 85 of the longer and most inspiring ones as material for the book. Khenchen Tsewang Gyatso had been Kyabje Penor Rinpoche's interpreter for the teachings, so with the support of his oral translation I produced a word-for-word translation from the recordings of the talks. Adapting oral teachings for publication in book form requires both sensitivity and familiarity with the material, and it was my editor Michael Tweed who took on the arduous task of molding these talks into a coherent whole by skillfully editing and arranging them into chapters. Of course, due to time and space restrictions, not all of Penor Rinpoche's comments could be included, but the pages that follow contain the primary topics of his message while accurately conveying Penor Rinpoche's unique tone and style.

I feel quite blessed to have had the opportunity to translate the profound instructions of this great master, which truly touch the core of one's heart. I have no doubt that merely reading these precious teachings will develop faith, devotion, and pure perception toward one's teacher and help clarify the view of the Great Perfection.

As for my personal experience with Drubwang Penor Rinpoche, my first

Drubwang Penor Rinpoche, empowerment at Namdroling Monastery, India
Photo © 2000 by Mannie Garcia

brief meeting with him was during the empowerments for the Treasury of Rediscovered Teachings (*Rinchen Terdzö*) that Kyabje Dilgo Khyentse gave at Mindrolling Monastery during the winter of 1978–79. A year or two later, I went to Namdroling Monastery, as Penor Rinpoche had invited Kyabje Dilgo Khyentse to transmit Longchen Rabjam's Four Branches of the Heart Essence (*Nyingtik Yabshi*), the Heart Essence Root Texts (*Nyingtik Tsapo*), and the Seven Treasuries (*Dzö Dun*). This occurred during the early years of Namdroling Monastery, when there were just a few buildings and Penor Rinpoche did everything himself: driving his car, going to the bank, doing the shopping, taking care of the young tulkus, and so forth—he seemed indefatigable. How he was able to accomplish so many activities is beyond me.

When I arrived there the first week of January 1980, I was very upset, as my main teacher, the eighth Khamtrul Döngyu Nyima Rinpoche, had

Drubwang Penor Rinpoche at Namdroling Monastery, India
Photo © 2000 by Mannie Garcia

suddenly passed away in Tongsar Dzong, Bhutan, where he was giving empowerments. Kyabje Dilgo Khyentse, who was in Nepal at the time, immediately went to Tongsar by helicopter to take care of the necessary rituals, after which Khamtrul Rinpoche's body was taken by car to his monastery at Tashi Jong in Himachal Pradesh, India. I'll never forget the extreme kindness Penor Rinpoche showed me during that time, while my heart was torn apart and unsure whether to wait for Kyabje Dilgo Khyentse or return to Tashi Jong to attend the ceremonies for my teacher. Every day I went to see Penor Rinpoche, who comforted me and advised me to wait for Dilgo Khyentse. It was very touching to watch him take care of everyone and everything in the monastery, including the laypeople in the village. Kyabje Dilgo Khyentse eventually arrived at Namdroling and said that he would personally perform Khamtrul Rinpoche's cremation on the forty-ninth day, so I felt great relief and stayed on to receive the empowerments.

Only a few hundred people were attending the empowerments, including a handful of foreigners. There was no guesthouse, so the monks vacated several rooms at the scriptural college, and we foreigners all had a comfortable place to stay. I'll never forget that time, as I rarely experienced such hospitality and kindness in a Tibetan monastery. At the end of the empowerments, which took about six weeks, we all went to Tashi Jong for

Drubwang Penor Rinpoche with Khenchen Tsewang Gyatso, monks, and
retreat students, Palyul Retreat Center, upstate New York
Photo © 2002 by Ursula Ward

Khamtrul Rinpoche's cremation, performed by Kyabje Dilgo Khyentse and
Tai Situ Rinpoche.

In 1986–87 Kyabje Dilgo Khyentse gave the transmission of Mipham
Rinpoche's Collected Works at Namdroling Monastery, and again I had
the great fortune to attend. During that period Kyabje Dudjom Rinpoche
passed away in France, so Kyabje Dilgo Khyentse went to France for the necessary ceremonies, and we all waited at Namdroling for him to return and
conclude the transmissions. During the week that Kyabje Dilgo Khyentse
was in France, Penor Rinpoche gave some special empowerments and transmissions of the Eight Commands (*Kabgye Desheg Dupa*) and the Embodiment of Realization (*Gongdu*). When Kyabje Dilgo Khyentse returned,
he completed the transmissions of Mipham Rinpoche's Collected Works.
During the concluding ceremonies, I was very moved when I noticed tears
of devotion streaming down Penor Rinpoche's face.

Several years later, I had the good fortune to interpret for Penor Rinpoche in Italy, where in 1993 he gave a week of empowerments and teachings
at Namkhai Norbu Rinpoche's Merigar center, which was a delightful event.

And a few years later, when Penor Rinpoche was invited by the Shambhala community in Amsterdam to give five days of empowerments and teachings, I was again invited to interpret; during that time he was so kind as to visit my apartment for dinner, which was a very joyful evening.

The forewords by Dzongsar Khyentse Rinpoche, Mugsang Kuchen Rinpoche, Sogyal Rinpoche, and Khenchen Tsewang Gyatso already relate Penor Rinpoche's extraordinary qualities and activities in great detail, so it's needless for me to add anything more here.

There are many blessings in being able to work with such precious material, and I pray that I've been able to present even a fraction of its profundity. May well-informed readers exercise restraint in the knowledge that the translator takes full responsibility for any errors, and may whoever encounters these teachings develop faith and inspiration to practice them. I pray to the buddhas, lineage masters, and Dharma protectors to forgive my inability to translate with perfect accuracy, as well as any mistakes of omission or commission in preparing this book. By the virtue of this work, may the Buddhist doctrine spread in the ten directions, may the lives of the lineage holders be stable and long, and may all beings attain happiness and enlightenment.

Tashi Jong, February 2017

ACKNOWLEDGMENTS

I WOULD LIKE TO thank everyone who has been involved in this project. First of all, my immense gratitude goes to the late Kyabje Penor Rinpoche for bestowing these exceptionally profound instructions, and to Khenchen Tsewang Gyatso for his oral translation as well as his inspiring foreword relating Penor Rinpoche's activities. My sincere gratitude goes to the sublime incarnations Dzongsar Khyentse Rinpoche, Sogyal Rinpoche, and Mugsang Kuchen Rinpoche for their outstanding forewords describing Kyabje Penor Rinpoche's amazing qualities in such a profound way. Heartfelt appreciation goes to Michael Tweed; without his skillful editing, this book could not have been published. My special gratitude goes to the Khyentse Foundation for their financial support and to John Ward, who requested the translation and without whom this project would not have been possible. I also thank Shambhala Publications for publishing this book and for the excellent work of their editors. Lastly, I am grateful to Khenpo Sonam Tsewang and Bill Speckart for their valuable corrections and suggestions, to Mannie Garcia for allowing me to use some of his remarkable photographs, and to Peter Woods for his careful reading of the manuscript and his insightful suggestions.

PART ONE

RECEIVING TEACHINGS

WHENEVER YOU RECEIVE Dharma teachings, you should conduct yourself in a humble way and generate the proper motivation: to liberate all beings from suffering. In the texts it says that you should remain like someone who is very humble and peaceful. You should be like a yak without horns—when a yak has horns, it's very proud and wants to fight everyone, but once its horns are cut or broken, it becomes very humble.

You should be free of the three defects of a pot: not listening, like an upside-down pot; not being able to retain what you hear, like a pot with a hole in it; and mixing negative emotions with what you hear, like a pot that contains poison. You should also avoid the six stains: pride, lack of faith, lack of effort, outward distraction, inward tension, and discouragement. These six stains are due to thinking that you are better than the teacher who is explaining the Dharma; not trusting the teacher or the teachings; failing to apply yourself to the Dharma; getting distracted by external events; focusing your five senses too intently inward; and being discouraged, for instance, if the teaching is too long.

In addition, you should avoid the five wrong ways of remembering: remembering the words but not the meaning, remembering the meaning but forgetting the words, remembering both but with no understanding, remembering them out of order, and remembering them incorrectly.

When receiving teachings, it is also important to engage in the six perfections: make excellent offerings, such as preparing the teacher's seat, arranging a flower offering, incense, and so forth, which is the practice of generosity; clean the place, put it in order, control your behavior, and listen with the proper motivation, which is the practice of discipline; do not harm even the smallest insect and bear heat, cold, pain, and other difficulties, which is the practice of patience; discard any wrong views concerning the teacher and the teachings and listen joyfully with genuine faith, which is the practice of diligence; listen to the teacher's instructions without distraction, which is concentration; and ask questions to clear up doubts and uncertainties, which is the practice of wisdom. Embraced by the six perfections, such conduct accumulates a vast amount of merit.

You should also generate the four types of faith, which are vivid, eager, confident, and irreversible faith. Among these, confident faith and irreversible faith are the most important. Vivid faith arises upon meeting a great master or visiting a temple with representations of the Buddha's body, speech, and mind. Eager faith is the eagerness to be free of the sufferings of the lower realms and engage in positive actions. Confident faith is the faith in the Three Jewels that arises from the bottom of one's heart. And irreversible faith is having such confidence that no matter what happens, your faith remains unshakable.

Lastly, you should consider the teacher as a skillful doctor, the teachings as medicine, yourself as the patient, and diligent practice as the treatment to recover from your illness.

It is extremely important that your mind be steadfast and your intention pure; without that, even your worldly activities cannot be successful. In one of his previous lives, Buddha Shakyamuni was a cowherd during the time of the third buddha of this era, Kashyapa. When Buddha Kashyapa came to his area, the cowherd boy felt fervent devotion and offered seven peas, which fell into Buddha Kashyapa's begging bowl. Due to the merit of that act, in his next life he became a universal king, and his seat was on the same level as Indra, king of the gods. This was due to his pure motivation and intention, not to the size of the offering.

Relying on a Master

WE ALL NEED to find freedom from samsara and attain enlightenment, and the only way to do so is by relying on a spiritual master, receiving the master's guidance, and practicing what the master teaches. All the past, present, and future buddhas rely on a teacher; there is not a single enlightened being who attains enlightenment without depending on a master. Nowadays, many people think that they can just do their own meditation without relying on a teacher, but that's not very beneficial, and when meditation is not successful, it may cause rebirth in the animal realm.

If enlightenment could be attained without reliance on a master, the buddhas and lineage masters of the past would have said so, but they all attained enlightenment by relying on their master and practicing his or her instructions. One may be a great scholar and memorize as many texts as an elephant can carry on its back, but one still won't attain enlightenment without the blessings of a master. It is through the blessings of one's guru that one can recognize the nature of one's mind. I'm not just making this up; that's how all the masters explained things.

It is said that it's important to have a connection with highly realized masters, whether it's a connection through Dharma or mundane matters and whether such a connection is positive or negative. If we can't have a positive connection with highly realized masters, then even with a negative connection, although we'll have to experience the result by wandering for a time in samsara, ultimately we will receive benefit because of such a master's power of bodhichitta. Even though there is no end to samsara for sentient beings in general, for those who have a connection with the Dharma, there will be an end. Thus, continuously pray to your master from the depths of your heart.

The Tibetan word for master is *lama*. *La* refers to unsurpassed, inconceivable wisdom and *ma* to the loving-kindness of a mother. So a master is someone endowed with inconceivable wisdom and boundless love for all beings.

When I mention the word *master*, maybe you think I'm talking about myself, but I'm just explaining the transmissions that the past masters taught and the related stories. Don't create too many concepts about what I myself am saying here; develop trust and confidence in what the past masters and buddhas taught, and generate faith and devotion in them. I personally don't have any experiences or realization at all and know nothing about what might happen tomorrow or next year or even what will happen tonight. I might not have any of the qualities or powers a master should have, but even so, without relying on a qualified master there is no way to attain enlightenment.

When Naropa was told by his teacher that his karmic root master was Tilopa, he set off to find him. He searched for a very long time, wandering far and wide, but couldn't find him anywhere. Finally, he asked someone if they knew where a master named Tilopa lived and was told that someone by that name was staying in a small house with smoke coming out the roof. When Naropa arrived, he found Tilopa grilling fish in the fire. Naropa asked Tilopa to accept him as his student and requested teachings, but Tilopa replied, "What are you talking about? I'm just a beggar!" But Naropa wasn't fooled and was certain that this was his master, so he followed him for twelve years, doing exactly what Tilopa told him to do.

One day they came to a high cliff and Tilopa said, "If you want to follow your master's command, jump off this cliff!" So Naropa went up to the cliff's edge and jumped. He ended up half dead with all his bones broken. When Tilopa came to see him three days later and asked if he was sick, Naropa replied, "I'm not just sick, I'm dying!" So Tilopa cured him through his blessings. In that way, Naropa experienced eighteen hardships but didn't receive any teachings. Then one day, while making tea, Tilopa sent Naropa to fetch some water. When Naropa returned with the water, Tilopa said, "No matter how much I tell you, you never understand!" Then he whacked Naropa very hard on the head with his sandal, knocking Naropa out. When Naropa regained consciousness, his realization had become equal to Tilopa's. This happened solely due to Naropa's fervent devotion to Tilopa.

There are countless stories of past great masters going through a lot of hardship while staying with their teacher. Here is a more recent example: Nyoshul Khen Rinpoche said that Khenpo Ngakchung was an emanation of Vimalamitra. The previous Drubwang Rinpoche (Palchen Dupa) studied philosophy with him and received all the pith instructions. One day, Khenpo Ngakchung said they should go for a stroll, and they went to an isolated place where Khenpo Ngakchung wanted to sit, so Drubwang Rinpoche took off his shirt and let Khenpo Ngakchung sit on it. Sometime after that, they went for another walk, and Khenpo Ngakchung got extremely angry. He took off his shoe and beat Drubwang Rinpoche so badly that Drubwang Rinpoche fell unconscious, and when he regained consciousness, his realization was equal to his master's. If one follows one's master with such strong and unwavering devotion, the result can really be quite extraordinary, but these days any master who did such things in the United States would likely be arrested and put in prison.

In fact, there are many practitioners who have realized the nature of mind and attained perfect enlightenment just by doing guru yoga. Being introduced to the nature of one's mind can happen only through the master's blessings, and without the blessings nothing will happen. This is not something that can be bought, and no matter how learned a scholar you may become, without a qualified master it's not possible to recognize the true nature of our mind. As this is the root of the practice, without blessings there is no way to attain enlightenment, and the path to buddhahood is blocked. There is no other way to discover the nature of your mind; you can't buy it or find it anywhere other than through the blessings of a qualified master. That is why the single most important practice in Dharma is guru yoga.

We have now obtained this precious human body endowed with the eighteen favorable conditions, which is very hard to obtain and may never be acquired again. If we use this support to practice Dharma and enter the path of liberation, we will always receive the proper support to continue on the path, but if we don't use it to integrate the Dharma into our being, there is very little chance of getting such an opportunity again. If we don't use our precious human body for Dharma practice, we may accumulate a lot of wealth, power, fame, and so on, but it will have no real benefit and will just carry us farther away from the path of liberation, casting us into the lower realms. Thus, it is our responsibility to strive again and again to let our master's blessings enter our stream of being. Now that we have obtained this precious human body, we should acknowledge, feel confident, and never forget that our sole object of refuge is the Three Jewels manifesting as our root master in the form of Guru Padmasambhava, who is the embodiment of all past, present, and future buddhas.

Our physical form really is extraordinary, so we should use our body, speech, and mind for the sake of perfect enlightenment, physically doing prostrations, circumambulations, and sitting in meditation; verbally reciting mantras and Dharma texts as much as we can; and mentally giving rise to bodhichitta, vast or small. All this is possible only because of this exceptional human form that came about through the kindness of our parents—without parents we wouldn't have a body, and without a human body we couldn't engage in virtuous practice. It is said that this body has great potential, both positive and negative: If we use it properly, we can accumulate a great deal of merit, but if we use it in a negative way, we can cause a great deal of harm. We can accumulate such negative actions that we'll never attain liberation, or we can engage in Dharma practice and attain perfect enlightenment in this very lifetime.

Please remember that beings in nonhuman forms such as gods, nagas, animals, gandharvas, and so forth don't have the opportunity to attain liberation, so now that you have obtained this extraordinary support, which is so rare and precious, and have been so fortunate as to meet the Dharma, you shouldn't waste such a rare opportunity; instead, devote yourself wholeheartedly not only to receiving teachings but to applying them as well.

FAITH, DEVOTION, AND DOUBT

THUS, WITH YOUR body, speech, and mind, you should develop faith and devotion toward your master, who embodies the buddhas of past, present, and future; supplicate your master from the depths of your heart; and, relying on guru yoga, receive direct introduction to the true nature of mind or, if that is not possible, then receive your master's blessings.

Whether those blessings enter your being depends not on the object of your devotion but on your own mind. We've all heard the story about the old lady who had incredible faith and devotion toward a dog's tooth, thinking that it was the Buddha's tooth. Though it was just a dog's tooth, she received the Buddha's blessings and attained enlightenment, which was due not to the tooth but entirely to her strong faith and devotion.

The enlightened mind of the buddhas is free of partiality, so whether you receive their blessings or not depends on the strength of your devotion and your dedication to your practice. For example, the sun always shines in the sky, but it is up to us to go outside and receive its warmth. If we continuously supplicate Padmasambhava with intense devotion, then he will not be somewhere far away on the Copper-Colored Mountain—he will always be right here, inseparable from us. Whether or not we see Padmasambhava, inseparable from our root master, depends upon our recognizing that he is inseparable from us, visualizing him on the crown of our head, and generating one-pointed faith and devotion toward him. Whether we are happy or unhappy, whether we have success or not in this life, where we are born in future lives, and ultimately whether or not we attain enlightenment all depends on our faith and devotion toward our teacher, who is inseparable from Padmasambhava. He is always present, so if we cannot see him, it is due to our own obscurations, negative emotions, and conceptual thoughts.

Once you have relied on a master, you should cultivate devotion, consider your guru to be the real Buddha, and pray to them. That is the only way to receive the master's blessings. Your teacher will explain the authentic Dharma teachings, and that is the path that will benefit you. It's important to examine the teacher at the very beginning, but to criticize your teacher after relying on them creates the negative karma of abandoning the Dharma. It's our karma to meet whatever teacher we meet, and if we follow our master's teachings and supplicate them as the real Buddha, we will be fine. Ordinary worldly people like us all have impure perception, and it's really difficult to have true faith and devotion. Even if we were to meet the actual Buddha face-to-face, we might still have wrong views. However, whenever you see fault in anything your sublime teacher does, you should feel deeply embarrassed and ashamed of yourself. At such times, you should reflect that such negativity is due to your own impure mental conceptions and that all your teacher's actions are utterly flawless and unerring, and thereby strengthen your pure perception and increase your faith.

For instance, the monk Sunakshatra was the Buddha Shakyamuni's half brother and served him for twenty-four years. He knew by heart all the twelve categories of teachings in the Pitakas, but he saw everything the Buddha did as deceitful. Eventually he came to the erroneous conclusion that, apart from an aura six feet wide, there was no difference between the Buddha and himself, so one day he told the Buddha, "Apart from the light around your body six feet wide, in twenty-four years as your servant I have never seen even a sesame seed's worth of special qualities in you. And as for the Dharma, I know as much as you—so I will no longer be your servant!" So saying, he left, and Ananda became the Buddha's personal attendant. When Ananda asked the Buddha what was going to happen to Sunakshatra, the Buddha replied, "In one week's time, Sunakshatra's life will come to an end. He will get thirsty and die from drinking some water, and then he'll be reborn as a hungry ghost in a flower garden." Ananda believed what the Buddha said and went to see Sunakshatra to relay it to him. Ananda advised Sunakshatra to be careful and to offer confession to the Buddha, but Sunakshatra thought to himself, "Sometimes those lies of his come true, so for seven days I had better be very careful. At the end of the week, I'll make him eat his words." So he spent the week fasting. On the morning of the seventh day, his throat felt very dry, so he drank some water, which made him sick and he died. Upon hearing this news, Ananda asked the Buddha where Sunakshatra was reborn, and the Buddha told him, "He was reborn in a flower garden as a hungry ghost with all the nine marks of ugliness, and after that he will be born again in the lower realms." Hearing this, Ananda asked the Buddha to liberate Sunakshatra, so the Buddha went to where Sunakshatra was born in a tree as a hungry ghost. There the Buddha gave him refuge and teachings on the law of cause and effect, but because of his wrong views Sunakshatra didn't listen to the Buddha's teachings and said, "During my time in the human realm you kept deceiving me, and even now that I've died you're still trying to deceive me!" So he wouldn't listen and, just as predicted, he was reborn in the lower realms.

The buddhas and bodhisattvas constantly watch and care for all sentient beings like a mother looking after her only child. They are without partiality and do not harbor attachment toward some and hatred toward others. If we have strong faith, devotion, and pure perception, the connection to receive their blessings will occur. When there are many fish in the water, it is possible to catch some with a net, but if there are no fish in the water, no matter how hard you try, you will never catch any. Similarly, if you cast the net woven from steady faith and devotion, you will "catch" some blessings, but without faith and devotion, there is no way for the blessings to enter your mind stream.

It is said that we shouldn't create doubts or wrong views, but rather train in pure perception. It is not to benefit the object of our devotion but for our own good that we are told to purify karmic obscurations, accumulate merit, and generate faith, devotion, and pure perception. Having doubts and wrong views about their accomplishment will not affect the qualities of the buddhas, bodhisattvas, and masters, and having faith, devotion, and pure perception toward them won't increase their qualities.

If we had pure perception from the beginning, we wouldn't need to train in it. However, at present our mind is filled with disturbing emotions, our way of perceiving is very obscured, and we lack pure perception. Therefore, we need to train in pure perception.

Furthermore, if we make a connection with a master, receive and practice the master's teachings, but then later think it's useless and give it all up, this will create a lot of obstacles, not for our teacher but for our own path of liberation. That's why training in pure perception and not creating wrong views is emphasized so much.

Nevertheless, even after committing ourselves to a teacher, we still tend to want to analyze the Buddhist teachings and our teachers because we're suspicious and feel uncertain. It's not that this is not allowed, but there is no need to do so and it has no benefit. When you first start out on the Buddhist path, it is necessary to check out teachers and question the teachings, but once you've entered the gate of the Dharma and have chosen a teacher, then to keep questioning, entertaining doubt, remaining uncertain, and being suspicious is considered a wrong view.

Of course, there are many different levels of teachers, but once you have taken a teacher, it's important to stay with that teacher. Having accepted a teacher, to then develop wrong views and criticize them is one of the greatest obscurations. If this does happen to you, then it is important to tame your mind and generate one-pointed faith and devotion so that you can receive your master's blessings.

Similarly, once you have entered the gate of the Dharma, don't waste your time examining whether the Buddhist teachings are true or whether they have blessings. Instead, analyze your own mind to see how much devotion, pure perception, doubt, and wrong concepts you have, and thereby subdue your own mind and become a suitable vessel for the blessings.

We may have all sorts of suspicions and wrong views, but these will only harm us; they won't affect Padmasambhava at all. On the other hand, thinking that we are so wise and learned may actually lead us to the hell realms. Since we are only here for a short time, if we have doubts and uncertainties and want to examine the Buddha's teachings minutely, we will end up without any time to practice them. As life is so short, we need to spend what little time we have generating faith and devotion and practicing one-pointedly, free of doubt. It is said that an unwavering mind can accomplish anything, and we surely can accomplish the Dharma if we dedicate ourselves to our practice and don't waver.

If you have very sincere devotion and inclination to practice the teachings free of any doubt, you'll definitely receive the blessings. We already have all the buddha qualities complete within us; they never decrease or increase. Because we don't recognize our true nature, however, we keep wandering in samsara. We're like a beggar who has a treasure vase underneath his bed but isn't aware of it, so he just goes on begging. But when the beggar meets someone who is aware of the treasure and actually shows it to him, then the beggar doesn't need to beg anymore, and his poverty and suffering are eliminated. Likewise, the moment the omniscient buddha nature present within all beings is actually seen and recognized, there is no longer any need to continue wandering in samsara.

Nowadays, scientists examine everything to discover its nature, but there is no physical surgery that can be performed to introduce us to our true nature. If you want an operation to be introduced to your true nature, you must wield the scalpel of faith and devotion and continuously practice without any hesitation or doubt.

If you doubt whether the masters and the lineage have blessings, you will not have much of a chance to receive blessings, and if you can't be liberated through the teachings of the Buddha, there is simply no other alternative. If there were another way, we could consider it, but there isn't one. There are many powerful gods and spirits, but though they may be able to control the world, they aren't liberated and are still wandering in samsara experiencing countless sufferings.

Thus, with steady devotion of body, speech, and mind, supplicate your master, who is the embodiment of all the buddhas appearing in the form of Padmasambhava. Feel confident that the compassionate blessings of your master's body, speech, and mind are transferred into your being. Because the blessings are being transferred to you, you can attain enlightenment. But this won't happen if you have doubts, lack genuine faith in your master, or are obscured by emotional thoughts. Those will only take you further away from enlightenment.

Once, two monks who were not very intelligent asked the previous Drubwang Rinpoche to tell them what practice they should dedicate their lives to. Drubwang Rinpoche told one monk just to chant a ten-page text known as the "Liberation through Touch from the Hundred Peaceful and Wrathful Deities" cycle, and he told the other monk just to recite the hundred-syllable Vajrasattva mantra. So they both spent their entire lives praying to their master and doing the practice that he had told them to do. I was about two or three years old when they passed away, and when the monk who had chanted the "Liberation through Touch" died, he remained in meditation while many rainbows appeared. When the monk who had spent his life chanting the hundred-syllable mantra was cremated, a rainbow appeared, as well as about a kilo of relics. Even though their knowledge was quite limited and they knew nothing about the practice of Dzogchen, the Great Perfection, these two simple monks attained accomplishment merely by praying to their master and obeying his instructions without a shred of doubt. Similarly, if you have faith and devotion and are inclined to practice the Great Perfection, each one of the 6,400,000 verses of the Great Perfection is a complete path leading to perfect liberation.

It is useless to have doubts as to whether the Dharma will have any benefit or can be accomplished, for all these Dharma teachings were composed and taught not by ordinary individuals but by sublime realized individuals who had attained complete accomplishment. If we indulge our doubts, we will not be able to accomplish anything, That's why I keep repeating over and over not to doubt but instead to have faith and devotion in your master and to dedicate yourself to your practice.

SAMSARA

EVERYONE IN THIS world wants perfect comfort and happiness. Not a single being wants to suffer. If we exert ourselves, we may be able to create a comfortable situation, but no matter what temporary comfort and happiness we achieve through our efforts and hardships, it's never steady or permanent. However, by practicing the Dharma, we can achieve the unsurpassed, ultimate bliss that liberates all from the sufferings of samsara and leads to perfect happiness.

Having been born in this world, we are attached to samsara, and being constantly preoccupied with our day-to-day survival, we experience a lot of hardship as we try to gather the necessary resources to spend our life in comfort. And so the years pass without our really accomplishing anything of lasting value. If we succeed in doing something or acquire some knowledge, we feel very arrogant about it, and when we don't succeed in doing what we wish, we worry about it day and night, and the stress of our worries makes us sick. Once we are sick, we focus on the illness, which only causes us to suffer even more. There is no benefit at all in being worried. It doesn't accomplish anything, nor does it purify our obscurations. Worry also doesn't help us acquire more wealth; it only increases our disturbing emotions and makes it that much more difficult for us to succeed. When our mind thinks too much, we accumulate a certain type of mental karma, and we're so accustomed to it that we can't stop worrying. Even when we know that worrying doesn't help, we still can't stop. So even though we need to engage in worldly jobs for the sake of our livelihood, we shouldn't be attached to them, but should cut our grasping to them.

Of course, it's important to take care of your finances and have some resources to support yourself, but you should not concentrate only on that. You should be satisfied with whatever you need for your livelihood and not keep amassing more and more. Remind yourself that between this life and your next, your next life is much more important. It's nice to have a few material belongings, but it's very rare for us to be content with what we have. Not only that, it's also difficult to keep what we have. People keep making more and more money, yet never feel that they have enough. According to the Dharma, if we possess wealth, we need to know how to use it. It's beneficial to have enough to support ourselves, not for pleasure's sake but so that we can focus more intently on our Dharma practice. What we really need is the Dharma, not more wealth, so it is best to concentrate on Dharma practice and be content having just enough to live on. Just look at how animals manage to survive. For example, in Tibet there is an animal that looks like a squirrel. During the summer it collects dry leaves and lines an underground burrow with them. Then it collects just enough of a nutritious type of grass called *dronma* to last the winter. It doesn't seek a fancy house or want more just for the sake of having more but is content with just what it needs to survive.

Nowadays, many Tibetans have the freedom to practice Dharma and are not tied down by a difficult financial situation like people in the West. In North America and Europe, you really need to have a job or you can't support yourself, so it's best not to waste your money but use it wisely. Many Tibetans go through a lot of trouble to get to the United States and to repay the debts they incurred in the process, and often they don't even have proper visas or permits. Yet, in spite of all that, they still manage to find a job, save money to pay their debts, and send some home to support their families. Most Americans, however, are born with so many advantages that they don't realize how fortunate they actually are. So please don't waste your money— use it for Dharma practice.

During our entire life we have been involved in so many activities, but if you really think about it, the result of wealth and fame is only temporary; it doesn't benefit our next life whatsoever but only causes negative karma. We may possess all the riches on earth, but when we die there is not so much as a blade of grass that we can take with us. On the other hand, our negative karma follows us like a shadow, even through the bardo after we die.

Now that you have obtained this precious human body that is so hard to find, try to make it meaningful by truly taking advantage of this rare opportunity. Worldly activities such as attaining high status, accumulating property and wealth, and so forth really have no benefit whatsoever, so please don't waste this precious opportunity. We may command a retinue of thousands of attendants and soldiers, but at the time of death we have to go alone, and at that time the only thing that can help is our own Dharma practice. So, from now on, don't get carried away by your thoughts and negative emotions but control and reduce them, supplicate the Three Jewels, and diligently apply yourself to your practice. I assure you that if you truly concentrate on your Dharma practice, it is possible to reach the highest levels of realization in this very lifetime, so you really don't need to wander in samsara anymore. But sadly, we humans tend to look at the world upside down and neglect what's most important, while perceiving trivial matters as the main purpose in life.

Once, when I was teaching in Taiwan, I told some students not to be attached to their jobs, but they said, "If we don't do our work, then who will?" But Taiwan won't come to a standstill just because a few people stop working. Actually, it's good if samsara becomes empty; if all beings attain liberation, we don't need samsara. We've been wandering here for countless lives and experience nothing but suffering. Our whole life is nothing but hardship and misery, but we still haven't accomplished anything, and even though we may plan a happy and comfortable life with our family, when the time comes to retire we say to ourselves, "Now I'm done with my job, and I'm going to relax." But instead, when we retire we worry about our savings, our health, and a thousand other things. We still hope that we can be happy and peaceful but end up dying without fulfilling our wishes, and often we experience a terminal illness that causes intense suffering. On the other hand, when bodhisattvas and realized masters die, it is always in a happy state of mind because they have attained freedom and are happy to go to the pure lands. They are not afraid but actually enjoy death.

Death and Impermanence

GENERALLY SPEAKING, THERE is nothing in this world that is stable or permanent, and just as the seasons continually change, everything is impermanent. From the moment we emerged from our mother's womb until now, everything has changed from one moment to the next. Even though we plan to make ourselves comfortable and cozy, it doesn't usually happen that way, does it? So don't expect any of the external or internal phenomena of this world to last. The more attachment you have to mundane things, the more your negative thoughts and unvirtuous actions will increase. So strive to reduce your attachment and clinging as much as you can, for no matter how hard you try to maintain things, at some point you'll have to let everything go anyway.

Whatever kind of worldly activity you get involved in for the sake of comfort, belongings, and wealth, it only takes you farther away from the path of omniscience and won't help you progress on the path. No matter how educated and wise you may be, everyone has to die, and at the time of death you'll be staring with frightened, wide-open eyes and gaping mouth, and yet there will be nothing you can do. At the time of death, worldly people still feel attached to their spouse, children, and property, so they die in a state of attachment. But if we practice correctly, we'll be able to reduce our attachment to our family and belongings and not feel attached when death arrives. If we practice Dharma, when we die we can ripen the qualities we have developed through our practice, and that will benefit us in our next life. Constantly try to focus on death and impermanence, resolve that nothing is permanent, and contemplate the sufferings of samsara. When you understand that all outer and inner phenomena of this world and its beings are impermanent and that your life is impermanent too, it will help turn your mind to the Dharma and inspire you to practice more seriously.

Except for the sacred Dharma, there is nothing else you can trust, no other refuge to rely on in this world.

When you die, you only take with you the negative actions that you have accumulated during this life and whatever positive, virtuous actions you've engaged in. That's all that follows; your body is left behind. From the buddhas and bodhisattvas above down to the tiniest insect below, there is no one who can escape death, and at the time of death there is no one who can help you. Though you may have many children, relatives, and friends, at the time of death you are on your own. Certainly they will show their love and affection and care for you, but there is little others can do for you when you die.

In the Tibetan tradition, when someone dies, the family will spend a lot of money for Dharma practice on their behalf, but no matter how incredibly wealthy you may be and no matter how kind your family, they won't spend all your money and possessions on your behalf. If you have $100,000, they might spend $30,000 to have rituals performed; the rest they'll keep for themselves.

The only thing that accompanies you across the threshold of death is the karma that you've accumulated from the negative actions of creating worldly success. It's important to contemplate this. In Tibet, there are many hunters who spend their entire life killing wild animals. At the time of death, before they stop breathing, lots of wild animals come and butt their heads against them, which creates great fear and suffering, so they ask others to chase them away. Some people with heavy negative karma feel like they are falling down at the time of death, and ask their caregivers to lift them up.

Some people who never practiced Dharma die instantly, and nowadays in the hospital people are given shots to die easily. For those who know nothing about Dharma, that seems to be a comfortable way to die, but for Dharma practitioners it's not a good way. We should be conscious and practice while dying.

In general, when people are dying, we should not touch them anywhere, because their consciousness may go wherever they are touched. It is said that when someone is about to die, lamas or monks can touch their heads or pillows, but nobody should touch them anywhere on their lower body. The seeds of the six realms of samsara are within our own body, so if touched on the lower body, the dying person might end up going to whichever of the six realms is related to that part of the body. Remember that karma always takes effect, and, unless it's properly confessed, it will accompany you until it ripens and is purified. So be kind to yourself and practice the Dharma while you have this rare opportunity.

None of us has any idea when we'll die or how. Once we become terminally ill, things get pretty difficult, but by then it's too late, and before we know it we're dead. If you think about this, you can prepare yourself and die at ease. As a Dzogchen practitioner who practices the preliminaries followed by the main practice, if you practice properly you should be able to attain liberation either within this lifetime or else in the bardo. As it stands, however, during the bardo after death, the peaceful and wrathful deities will manifest to liberate you, but due to your negative karma you won't perceive them as yidam deities; instead, you will be terrified. When the white, red, yellow, blue, and green lights of the five buddhas and five dakinis appear, you will perceive them as enemies and weapons that have come to harm you, and you will have no idea that they manifest to benefit you. However, if you could just recognize them as your own experience of the yidam deities, you would be liberated instantly. So, if you train yourself in Dharma practice now, it will really help, and you will then be able to recognize them and be liberated right there and then.

Due to their strong attachment to their wealth, as well as having gathered a lot of negative karma, many people suffer a lot of pain when dying. They cannot let go, and they die with great difficulty, gasping for air. But good Dharma practitioners who have attained freedom don't experience any suffering at death, and practitioners with a good heart who are always kind to others don't have much trouble when they die. Many just pass away while they're talking, smiling, and laughing.

In Namdroling Monastery there was an old lama named Lama Songlu. One day, even though he appeared to be in very good health, he said that he would die within the year. Soon after that, he got a little sick. When some students asked him how he was, he said he was fine but that if he did die he would just be moving from one house to another. He said not to worry about him and gave a lot of advice to people who came to visit, telling them not to get carried away by their disturbing emotions, to practice the Dharma, not to be attached to their family, to live in harmony, not quarrel, and so forth. Many people requested him to live a long life and not pass away, so they offered to take him to the hospital for treatment, but he said it was useless and refused to go. Traditionally in Tibetan culture, when someone dies, we make offerings to the lamas and monasteries to dedicate the merit in that person's name, so over the next three months Lama Songlu gave away all his belongings to masters all over India and got receipts for them. Then he asked the monastery to do the hundred-deity practice a thousand times, and when it was completed he came and made the customary offerings to the participants. After someone dies, we usually do rituals for seven weeks, and so he set aside money for these as well as for the cost of his cremation, leaving everything neatly prepared. He said that he didn't really need all this done for him, but since this was the tradition, he wanted to do things accordingly. Even though he was a very good lama who knew exactly what to do, people still criticized him because our worldly minds constantly follow conceptual thoughts and have no stability whatsoever. Many people didn't have much confidence in him, and throughout all this they were very skeptical, saying, "That lama should die now, otherwise what's the use of all this?" One day, as he thought his old clothes were quite dirty, he washed those he wasn't wearing and threw them in the fire. Then figuring that people would find his corpse filthy, he took a shower. The next day he passed away peacefully and painlessly.

About a year before the Chinese communists started to make trouble, my precious root master, Palyul Choktrul Rinpoche, told his disciples that he was going to pass away and asked them to prepare for it. Hearing this, all the tulkus and lamas went to see him to request him not to pass away and offered elaborate rituals for his longevity, so he said, "I do feel that this is the right time for me to die, but because you are insisting that I stay, I will live until you feel content." About two years later, the Chinese communists actually arrived. They arrested Choktrul Rinpoche and imprisoned him in a small prayer-wheel house. Later they took him to a prison far away, where he was kept in a room with a few other high lamas. One morning at breakfast, one of the other lamas said, "A few years ago you were going to pass away, but at the request of your students you didn't. However, now, as the Chinese will be torturing us, it seems like a good time to go." Hearing this, Choktrul Rinpoche replied, "Back then I thought that was a good time to pass on, so that the monastery could do the proper cremation and offering ceremonies, but as they requested me to remain, I did, and now there is no chance for any of that." Later that day, during lunch break, he suddenly died. He didn't commit suicide or hang himself; he just passed away while remaining in a state of omniscient wisdom. Over the following weeks, the other lamas also passed away one after the other, and nobody could take proper care of their bodies, as the Chinese took them away and buried them in some unknown place.

Many years later, when some of Choktrul Rinpoche's students wanted to recover his body, they didn't know exactly where he was buried, but they found a place that looked likely, so they erected a pillar on the spot. Later, when they started rebuilding the temple, they met someone who told them where the body was in fact buried, so they went to exhume the corpse in order to bury it properly. Upon digging up the earth, they found some pieces of the clothes he was wearing when he had passed away, and the area was very oily and filled with tiny relic pills.

Outwardly, these two great masters seemed to be ordinary lamas, but they spent their entire lives doing practice, and when they passed away, they displayed very special signs. So please take to heart how important it is to continuously reflect upon death and impermanence and maintain a meaningful practice. Remember that at the time of death you can only be liberated if you have trained in mingling your mind with your master's during this life. So you should continuously mingle your body, speech, and mind with your master's and remain in that nature of inseparability for as long as you can. It's very important to train in this again and again, and also to mingle appearances and mind without getting caught up in conceptual thoughts. If you don't become accustomed to doing this now, you will get carried away by your thoughts and will be in real trouble when the time comes to face your death. If you are attached to your family and possessions and worry about them when dying, you will get very scared during the intermediate state and will end up wandering in the three lower realms once again, but if you train and become stable in your practice now, constantly doing guru yoga, you won't be frightened throughout the stages of dying. So instead of getting carried away by conceptual thoughts, mingle your mind with your teacher's and perceive him as being inseparable from the essence of all the buddhas of the past, present, and future, Padmasambhava.

KARMA AND MERIT

EACH AND EVERY being in this world, including animals and all other beings of the six realms, wants to be happy. Nobody wants to suffer. Even though we have no wisdom or clairvoyance, we can see that everyone in this world is afflicted with disturbing emotions and delusion based on their karma—not only we humans, but all beings of the six realms. Even a tiny little ant is constantly afflicted by the five poisons, and it's impossible for such a being to generate bodhichitta, faith, devotion, or pure perception for an instant. It can't even conceive of a path to liberation or ultimate happiness. Due to karma accumulated throughout beginningless lifetimes, all sentient beings experience various kinds of sorrow and happiness. Yet this isn't just random, for all that we experience is the result of our past actions. So it's very important to be acutely aware of the law of cause and effect and to be extremely careful in all that we do.

Some people might think that if one does something negative or engages in positive actions, the result should be evident immediately, just as when you pull the trigger of a gun, the bullet hits the target right away, but that is not the case. In most cases, karma ripens over time, whether that happens to be in this life, the next life, or any of those that follow.

During the Cultural Revolution in Tibet, even though many people engaged in incredibly negative actions, they didn't suffer the fruition of their actions right away, so some people began to doubt the law of cause and effect. Many of them were given high-ranking positions by the Chinese government and gained great status, so they felt very proud. However, later, some of those who were involved in the most negative acts got very strange illnesses, and though the communist regime tried to treat them, they couldn't be cured, and most of them died within ten or fifteen years. In the beginning, a lot of young army people, following orders, were heavily involved in the Cultural Revolution, but later they realized that they had committed incredibly negative actions and felt regret about killing many beings and destroying temples and statues. When they got older, unable to bear their mental suffering, many committed suicide. But no matter how badly those people suffered, it can't compare to the suffering they are to experience in their future lives.

Consider the life story of Milarepa: the negative karma he accumulated by killing many beings and destroying many crops through the practice of black magic could only result in his going to the lower realms. When he realized his mistakes and started following his teacher Marpa, even though he was accepted as his student, he didn't receive one word of teaching but spent many years building houses for Marpa, undergoing incredible hardships. While Milarepa was building a huge nine-story house without any help, Marpa's son was nearby playing with a huge rock, and it rolled down toward the building site, so he used it for the foundation. Later on, when he was building the second story, Marpa came by and asked where he got the big rock, so Milarepa answered that Marpa's son had been playing with it, and when it rolled down he used it for the foundation. Marpa said that his sons were all realized emanations of bodhisattvas and shouldn't be Milarepa's servants, so he told Milarepa to put the rock back where it came from. Milarepa had to take the foundation apart and start again from scratch. When Marpa passed by again later, he told Milarepa to get the rock and put it in the foundation after all. Milarepa used to carry the stones on his back, and after some time his back turned into one big open sore. Then he started carrying the rocks in front, and his chest became full of open wounds. So it was that Milarepa spent years building and knocking down houses for Marpa. It wasn't that Marpa needed houses or had no one else to build them for him. All his demands were merely to purify Milarepa's negative karma.

Throughout the years, whenever Milarepa tried to attend a teaching that Marpa was giving, Marpa would get very angry and kick him out. One day Lama Ngokpa requested a Chakrasamvara empowerment and Milarepa really wanted to attend, so Marpa's wife, Dakmema, gave him a big piece of turquoise as an offering and told him to go to the empowerment. When Milarepa offered the turquoise during the empowerment, Marpa noticed that it was his wife's and asked who had given it to him or if he had stolen it. Milarepa answered that Dakmema had given it to him, so once again Marpa got furious and kicked him out of the room. He also scolded Lama Ngokpa as well as his wife. In the end, though Milarepa had accumulated a lot of negative karma, by obeying his teacher's commands and following his instructions he was able to purify his karma, and in doing so he became one of the most renowned, realized yogis in Tibet.

We've been wandering in the six realms of samsara since beginningless time, experiencing countless births and deaths, but due to our karmic obscurations we cannot see those past lives. If we could, there's no way we would be relaxing and sitting around as if we had plenty of time. We may not believe in or understand anything about past lives, but the Dharma teachings clearly explain the law of cause and effect, and our teachers also explain it over and over. Many people claim that there is no such thing as past and future lives or cause and effect, but not believing in the law of cause and effect isn't going to help anyone. It's the nature of phenomena that everything happens according to the law of cause and effect.

Some exceptional bodhisattvas take birth in the six realms in order to generate awareness about Dharma among the sentient beings living there, so that they can give rise to good qualities. In the life stories of the buddhas, we find that many of them emanated in that way. Mingyur Dorje could remember about five hundred of his past lives, and there are many stories about them. In my monastery in Kham, we used to have fifteen huge thangkas painted with gold depicting events from Mingyur Dorje's lives. In some of the thangkas, he is depicted as a frog benefiting frogs, in others as a bird guiding birds on the path of liberation; in some he is born as an insect benefiting insects and guiding them on the path of liberation, and in others he is depicted as a sheep benefiting sheep and trying to lead them to liberation. Sometimes he was born in the hells to liberate hell beings by teaching the Dharma. Some hell beings are so negative that it's very difficult to liberate them, because they can't give rise to even the tiniest bit of faith and devotion, so Mingyur Dorje would bless the sand and stones of the hells with mantras in order to extinguish the hell fires and benefit them in that way. The realms and types of sentient beings are countless and inexpressible, but we ourselves were born as human beings who can speak, hear, and understand, and this is the result of great merit.

The reason we wander in samsara is that we experience the karmic results of our previous actions, and until we've purified all karmic obscurations, we won't be able to attain enlightenment. The Dharma is taught solely so that all beings can purify the karmic obscurations that they have gathered throughout countless lifetimes in order to attain perfect enlightenment. So instead of putting a lot of effort into trying to attain temporary happiness, it would be much better just to accumulate merit by engaging in virtuous actions. Just as a blazing fire is ignited by a small spark, each small virtuous act naturally leads to true happiness. Buddha Shakyamuni gave 84,000 different teachings, and when teaching the Secret Mantrayana he taught innumerable tantras in order to purify our karmic obscurations and tame our minds. In the Secret Mantrayana there are many extremely skillful methods for accumulating merit, such as refuge, bodhichitta, mandala offerings, guru yoga, yidam practice, mantra recitation, and so forth. The Dzogchen teachings are the essence of all the Secret Mantrayana teachings and are said to swiftly purify our karmic obscurations so that we may attain enlightenment in this very body and lifetime.

Wherever there are sentient beings in this world, there is suffering—happiness is very rare. We hear about how difficult it is to obtain a precious human body, and if we really contemplate this, it seems almost impossible to find such an opportunity. When our parents were in union, countless beings tried to insert their consciousness into our mother's womb in order to obtain a body, and it was only due to our karmic connection with our parents that we could enter our mother's womb.

It is taught in the texts that the number of beings in the hell realms is equal to the particles of dust in this world, that the number of beings in the hungry ghost realm is equal to the number of snowflakes falling in a big snowstorm, and that in the animal realm the number of beings is equal to the grains of sand in a large river. There are innumerable tiny germs that we cannot perceive with our naked eyes; even the water we drink is full of tiny living creatures. So there's no way we can have any idea how many sentient beings there are, and each of these beings, whether we see them or not, has the five disturbing emotions. So to obtain a precious human body in such a world as this is of immense value, and the most important thing for us is to not waste such a precious opportunity but progress on the path of liberation.

The texts tell us that the enlightened qualities of the buddhas are within us; therefore, if we really make an effort in our practice, we can ripen that potential, reveal those qualities, and attain the result, enlightenment. It's similar to planting a fruit seed: If we properly tend it with the right soil, giving it the right amount of warmth and moisture, the seed will grow into a tree, and we can enjoy the fruit. Yet, no matter how well we nurture the earth, without a seed nothing will grow. Likewise, since buddha nature is within us from the very beginning, when we attain enlightenment we're not gaining anything new; rather, our inner qualities are awakened as we purify our obscurations and accumulate merit and wisdom. For instance, though the sun is always shining, we cannot see it when there are clouds. Similarly, though the inner qualities of an enlightened buddha are present within us, they're obscured by disturbing emotions. That's why we must purify our obscurations and accumulate merit and wisdom: so that these qualities can be revealed, just as the sun appears when the clouds disperse.

At present we cannot see properly—our perception is distorted, but by training in pure perception, we start to see things as they actually are according to their absolute nature. Don't get caught up with samsaric life; realize that it has no essence, and at all times try to develop faith and devotion. If we can develop our inner qualities, our attachment to samsara will naturally subside. Don't entertain doubt or hesitation, for they are like a net you cannot get out of. In this way, at all times, supplicating your root guru with your body, speech, and mind and mingling your mind with your guru's enlightened mind, remain in that state of inseparability, and without fabricating anything at all, just rest in the natural state.

EMPTINESS

ALL SAMSARIC PHENOMENA are compounded, and anything that's compounded is impermanent. We may think that the physical body of those we love is very beautiful, but when we analyze our attachment to it, we see that the physical body is nothing but a skeleton covered with flesh. The Dharma has many different methods to tame our mind, and the point of all these practices is to liberate our mind from attachment and aversion to compounded phenomena, as well as from conceptualization and clinging to the dualistic notion of subject and object. For example, in the Secret Mantrayana, we visualize all beings as mothers and sisters or as male and female deities, who are beyond thoughts of attachment or aversion.

The five poisons, our afflicting emotions, are coemergent from the time we were born. In the Hinayana tradition, practitioners try to abandon afflictive emotions like poison and have many methods to do so. In the Secret Mantrayana, all phenomena are sealed in the nature of emptiness, and when we abide in that nature, free of subject and object, the afflicting emotions cannot arise.

The outer and inner nature of phenomena is primordially pure emptiness, and from that state of emptiness anything can arise. All phenomena are emptiness, and from within emptiness all phenomena of samsara and nirvana appear. Because of emptiness and the interplay of interdependent circumstances, endless phenomena can arise within samsara and nirvana. When thinking of emptiness, you shouldn't imagine it as total voidness. That is a great mistake, for the nature of emptiness manifests as phenomena, while the nature of phenomena appears as emptiness—they are nondual. Emptiness and phenomena are not separate and are entirely within the nature of our own mind; there is nothing outside of that. Even gods, demons, spirits, and so forth, whether with form or formless, are primarily the display of our own minds, and mind itself is emptiness—not just voidness but emptiness free of all extremes. If you think emptiness is mere voidness, you misunderstand it. Emptiness is without elaboration and beyond any extremes, total simplicity; mere voidness is like a barren woman's child or a flower growing in the sky—they are nonexistent. As Nagarjuna said, "If they meditate on emptiness but don't have the correct understanding of emptiness, even intelligent people will fall into an abyss." Instead of leading toward liberation, such a view will lead to downfalls, so it's useless to concentrate on mere emptiness.

Whatever we perceive in this world—mountains, rocks, rivers, men, women, buildings, and so forth—none of it has a truly existing nature; nothing is real. As phenomena do not have a truly existing nature, there is no need to view them as substantial. We don't have to prove the existence of phenomena; simply by being perceived they are already affirmed. However, the reason we're still wandering in samsara is our attachment to phenomena as truly existing. As followers of the Dharma, we seek to see things as they actually are, not how we fantasize them to be. Yet we tend to spend our time in such meaningless ways, establishing phenomena the way we like to see them rather than as they actually are. For example, long ago in Varanasi there was an old lady whose meditation consisted of visualizing that she was a tigress. After she had been practicing many years, since she believed she was a tigress, everyone else saw her that way too. When she went to town, everyone was so scared that they all fled!

Everything is emptiness, but that emptiness is not mere voidness like space without anything. Even animals meditate on mere voidness: certain types of bears and marmots do voidness meditation throughout the winter. Also, during winter in Tibet, whole flocks of parrots stay inside huge empty, rotten trees and similar places near water and meditate on voidness. They don't eat anything, yet still they survive. But for us it is said that if we think of emptiness as mere voidness, then when we die we may be reborn in the related formless realm. In one of Mingyur Dorje's writings, there is a story about a non-Buddhist who only meditated on mere voidness and claimed that everything was void, so when he died and was taken to the hell realm, he was still saying, "There are no hells or hell beings—everything is void." So be aware that if you engage in meditation on mere voidness, that could happen to you too.

All the interdependent phenomena of samsara and nirvana are inseparable from emptiness. That is the meaning of appearances and emptiness being inseparable. Great emptiness is free from conceptual elaboration and free of limitation, so whatever your mind clearly thinks or visualizes can be accomplished accordingly, and within that emptiness all interdependent phenomena arise. Once, when Milarepa and some of his students were traveling, they camped in an open plain. A huge hailstorm suddenly came up, so they all ran for shelter. After the hail stopped falling, they looked everywhere but couldn't find Milarepa. Then someone heard singing coming from inside a yak's horn. They looked and there was Milarepa sitting inside the yak's horn, singing a song of realization. Milarepa's body hadn't shrunk and the horn hadn't gotten any bigger, but he was sitting comfortably inside it. Because of emptiness and interdependent phenomena, such things can happen. We always cling to things as being concrete and solid, so it is not possible for us to do such things, but since the outer universe and inner phenomena are all emptiness, such things are possible.

Because they realized the unity of emptiness and interdependent origination, the great masters of the past could walk through walls, traverse rocks and mountains unobstructed, leave handprints and footprints in solid stone, and perform various other kinds of miracles. At Palyul Monastery in Tibet, there was a lama named Tulku Langpal, who was imprisoned by the Chinese and bound in iron chains. Since the chains were very uncomfortable, he used to just slip out of them. When the prison guards came to check on him and saw that his chains were off, they scolded him, so he would instantly slip them back on. Sometimes he would just walk out of prison through the walls and stay outside, and when the guards came he would just pass through the wall and go back inside. For the sake of sentient beings, such great masters appear in many different ways; they have attained complete freedom. But we sentient beings always think everything is permanent and concrete. That's why we can't walk through solid walls but just bang into the bricks. The union of emptiness and interdependent arising pervades the whole of saṃsara and nirvana, and all the great masters can do such miraculous things due to that union of emptiness and interdependent arising. Just sitting in meditation they perceive everything that happens around them, but they have no attachment to it.

So what we need to do is train in emptiness, recognize that the nature of phenomena is empty, and realize that nature of emptiness within ourselves—this is what's important. Instead of conceptualizing about appearances, we should realize the primordial nature of emptiness and leave them in that nature. The way we perceive phenomena depends entirely on our karma, so we should give up clinging to the reality of these phenomena. We shouldn't deceive ourselves by thinking that samsara is permanent and something good. When we dream at night, we're not aware that we're dreaming; we see so many places and people and perceive them as real, but when we wake up, it's all gone. All present appearance is nothing but a dream, but if we really contemplate the nature of phenomena, we'll understand that anything compounded is impermanent and subject to change. If we give up clinging to samsara and, without contriving, realize appearances to be emptiness, we can attain enlightenment.

If there were just mere voidness, what would be the point of doing Dharma practice? Fortunately, that is not the case: all interdependent phenomena of samsara and nirvana arise from emptiness, and therefore we practice virtue and avoid misdeeds. Worldly people, non-Buddhist practitioners, and Buddhist practitioners of the nine vehicles all meditate on emptiness, but there are different ways of coming to a definite conclusion about emptiness. Whether the capacity emerges or not depends on realizing this fact in our very experience. However, the Great Perfection is the summit of all vehicles, and if we correctly meditate on primordially pure simplicity, it is possible to attain the ideal result.

Emptiness is beyond all extremes of existence, nonexistence, both, and neither, and resting your mind in a relaxed state, you approach that uncontrived state of emptiness. Experiencing the total simplicity of emptiness occurs mainly through faith, devotion, and pure perception toward the master, receiving the master's instructions, and gradually going through the practices. That's how you can start to experience genuine emptiness and be introduced to the nature of your mind. It's only through your devotion and the master's blessings that you can recognize the total simplicity of emptiness—there is no other way to realize it. If you rest in the uncontrived natural flow of mind, then you are approaching the right path.

Emptiness is always present, so not giving rise to thoughts and just relaxing free of thoughts has great benefit. On the other hand, thinking of emptiness as just voidness and meditating on that has some danger, as it can result in birth in the animal realm or the god realms where there are no concepts or feelings. But just resting without giving rise to thoughts has no faults, and your body, speech, and mind become very relaxed and joyful.

All the past buddhas and bodhisattvas recognized the nature of their mind and then attained enlightenment—there is no other way. I hope that you too will recognize your true nature, but to recognize the nature of mind is not so easy. Most people have to go through many hardships to be able to realize it. Please don't lose courage if you haven't yet recognized the nature of your mind. It cannot be stressed enough that the most important practice for recognizing your true nature is guru yoga, for it is only through your master's blessings that you can recognize emptiness. We already possess this nature. It's not something that needs to be fabricated or acquired from outside, so as you train your mind through faith, devotion, and pure perception, your disturbing emotions will gradually diminish, and then you will recognize your true nature.

BUDDHA NATURE

THE BUDDHA'S OMNISCIENT wisdom has been within every sentient being from the very beginning. Once, two merchants who were close friends sailed out to sea in search of wish-fulfilling gems. They both found one, and upon returning home, they enjoyed great wealth and happiness. One of them was married and had many children, but after he died his family gradually lost their wealth and became very poor. They eventually ended up having to support themselves by begging. One day, in search of alms, they came to the house of the other merchant, their father's friend, who immediately recognized them. He was very surprised to see their condition and asked why they were begging when their father had owned a wish-fulfilling gem. They told him that since their father died, they gradually lost all their wealth and were now very poor. He asked what their father had left behind, and they explained their house was empty—none of his belongings remained. So the merchant accompanied them back to their place to see if he could find a way to help them. Knowing how wealthy his friend had been, he was surprised to see the house practically empty, but he looked around and noticed a stone under the bed. Recognizing this as the wish-fulfilling gem, he pulled it out, cleaned and polished it, put it on the shrine, and told the family to supplicate it. They did as he instructed, and soon their wealth was restored and they no longer lived in poverty. We too already possess the wish-fulfilling gem of self-existing wisdom, so not only do we not need to suffer, but we also do not need to create anything.

The five poisons and disturbing emotions, in particular the net of doubt, have obscured us throughout beginningless lifetimes. Just like a beggar wandering around, we wander in samsara, constantly giving rise to disturbing emotions and dualistic thoughts from one life to the next. Such continuous dualistic thinking, holding on to a self where there is none, only increases our disturbing emotions, both subtle and gross. Dualistic thinking and ego-clinging are what mask our true nature, and though we understand that these are delusions and detrimental, we do not seem able to get rid of them immediately or on our own. It's only through our master's compassionate blessings that we can cut through our doubt and delusions to see our true nature as it is. That's why we need to pray to our master, and through the blessings of the Three Jewels, we can gradually reduce our disturbing emotions so that experience and realization can unfold.

The fact is that we don't have to go elsewhere to search for our own nature, for it is already within each and every one of us. And our buddha nature is exactly the same as that of the completely enlightened buddhas, as well as that of the tiniest insect—there is not the slightest difference between them. It is just that, like the sun shining in the sky becoming obscured by clouds, our buddha nature became obscured by our dualistic thinking and emotional afflictions. Nevertheless, if we rely on a master and practice the Dharma, especially the teachings of the Great Perfection, the master will introduce us to the natural state as it is. So always trust your master with total confidence, generating faith and devotion, pleading, "Look upon me with compassion!" You don't always need to see your master; just because you are apart doesn't mean that you won't still receive the master's blessings. There are many stories and biographies in which we find a master telling a student, "We have been inseparable from the very beginning, but due to your karmic obscurations, you couldn't see it." So be confident that your root master has always been inseparable from your body, speech, and mind, and practice accordingly.

Applying the Teachings

THE MOST IMPORTANT thing is to have faith and trust in the Buddha's words. The Buddha's teachings were not taught to deceive us but to explain the way things actually are. Many people try to analyze the Buddha's teachings, but how is it possible to scrutinize a buddha's qualities? We don't even know what will happen tomorrow, or when we will die, or anything about our future lives, so how could we possibly examine the teachings of the Omniscient One? Since we are totally obscured by our strong disturbing emotions, in order to progress on the path toward enlightenment, we have no choice but to have faith in the Buddha's teachings and apply them in our own lives.

The ability to practice Dharma depends on certain conditions. For example, this is a rare time during which the teachings of the Great Perfection are said to flourish. We're very fortunate that through Padmasambhava's blessings, such teachings have appeared and we're able to receive them. We must have accumulated incredible merit and made fervent prayers very sincerely over numerous lifetimes to be able to encounter such amazing teachings now. Still, most people are just too involved in worldly activities to have time to practice the Dharma, and very few people in this world totally dedicate themselves to the teachings. Most people work for the sake of success in this life, to gain wealth, fame, power, and so on, but none of these worldly aims can liberate us from the suffering of samsara; in fact, they only create further conditions for ensuring that we remain in samsara for countless lifetimes to come.

Dharma is not just something to study—it must be put into practice. These days, most people study Dharma for a little while and then start to teach it to others, thinking they have a certain depth of realization; however, without the realization that arises through practice, one doesn't actually know much at all.

This can't be stressed enough: Dharma must be applied! By properly practicing over the years—your whole life, in fact—you can attain some accomplishment. If you are hungry, just talking about food and describing how delicious it tastes will not fill your stomach, but if you actually prepare a meal and eat it, your hunger will be satisfied. Similarly, just talking about the Dharma will not lead you to enlightenment. Just as eating food is necessary to satisfy your hunger, the teachings you receive must be applied to have any effect.

There's a saying in Tibetan: "Someone who has a great deal of knowledge may become very proud, and someone who does a great deal of meditation practice may have strong afflicting emotions." That is what happens when someone goes against the Dharma and doesn't integrate their mind with the teachings. The spiritual path should be mingled with your mind stream to awaken your true nature; it should not be a source for boasting about your knowledge or experience. You can see by people's conduct—the way they talk and walk, whether they are proud or humble, and whether they have tamed their emotions or not—if they really practice or not. If someone is very calm and doesn't have many negative thoughts and emotions, that is a sign of a good practitioner. The more understanding of the Dharma one has, the more humble one should be; the more meditation one has done, the fewer disturbing emotions one should have.

Please remember that whether your studies and practice are effective or not depends on how much you actually integrate them into your life. At all times, try to watch your own mind to see how much your thoughts and conduct are in accord with the teachings. It's very easy to notice someone else's faults and criticize their practice, but instead you should turn your attention to your own thoughts and behavior. It is very important to watch your own mind and check how much you really apply the practice—just look at how many emotions come up in the span of a few seconds! We constantly get carried away with worldly activities and distractions, spending time with our family and friends and working at our jobs; all this exhausts us and takes up our time, so we end up neglecting our Dharma practice. We tend to make the less important concerns the most important in our life, but the most important thing in this world is to practice Dharma until we attain ultimate enlightenment, isn't it? Having food and clothing is a short-term necessity for this life, but we get so involved in our attachment to these things that we squander what little time we do have. We consider trivial matters more important than our Dharma practice, but when death comes, only practice will be of any benefit.

Now that we have obtained this precious human body, we should be sure not to squander this opportunity. There is no question that the sublime Dharma is far more important than mundane, worldly life. Mundane activity is bound to lead us to the lower realms. But if we sincerely engage in Dharma practice, we will be naturally guided to liberation and never to the lower realms. In particular, Dharma practice can get rid of our strong ego-clinging and afflictive emotions.

But getting rid of those is not like just peeling off your clothes and throwing them away. You've been cultivating your afflictive emotion for beginningless lifetimes, so unless you persevere in your practice for a very long time, it won't be easy to reduce your afflictions and attachments. However, if you continuously practice in a steady manner, generating bodhichitta, faith, and devotion without any doubts, you can gradually progress.

You need to stabilize your Dharma practice by focusing on one practice with one-pointed mind. Dharma has to be practiced from the depths of your heart with great perseverance and in a very steady way, or it won't be effective. Your practice has to be stabilized with stoutness of heart. In Tibetan, the term is *nying ru*, which literally means "heart bone." It is said that when a courageous warrior dies, because he has been constantly at battle throughout his life, a small bone is found in his heart. Likewise, many practitioners with strong perseverance and diligence in the practice also have such stoutness of heart. Without that kind of perseverance, it will be hard to achieve any accomplishment.

Fortunately, the compassionate Buddha gave different levels of teachings to suit each person's capacities and said, "My teaching has no owner and anyone can practice it; whether they are a king or a beggar, of high or low birth, rich or poor, beautiful or ugly, young or old, anyone who feels inspired and wishes to genuinely practice can attain ultimate happiness by correctly practicing my teachings."

The Dharma is extremely vast, and the practices are as numerous as the stars in the sky, but thinking that one practice is better than another will only increase your concepts. It is like a child who picks a pretty flower only to throw it away as soon as she sees another one. If you continually discard one practice for another, you won't be able to progress. It might be good to know many Dharma practices, but we don't have time to practice them all, so it's better to settle on one practice and stick with it to the end.

In the sutras, it is said that your Dharma knowledge may be as vast as all the volumes an elephant can carry on its back, but if you don't apply it, you won't be liberated. In Tibet, we have an animal called *dremong*, a type of brown bear. They usually dig in the earth and catch groundhogs in the forest and then kill them for their winter food. When they catch a groundhog, they sit on it so that it won't escape. But when they get up to catch another one, the first one escapes. So though this bear might catch eight or nine groundhogs, most of them escape and it has just one left to eat. It's the same with Dharma practice: you might know a little, but if you go off and chase one teaching after another, you will forget what you have already received and won't apply it. Then there's no benefit and the teaching becomes meaningless. Instead of chasing after teachings, you should apply what you have received and constantly train in it.

What is more, even though they have no realization, many people think that they can teach others what they have learned. Although you may have received many empowerments and teachings, unless you have stabilized your practice, there can be no benefit in your teaching others. Only once you've stabilized your practice can there be any benefit in teaching. Just supplicating a stone will not give you jewels, but supplicating a wish-fulfilling gem can fulfill all wishes, and if you practice the Dharma correctly, you can become a wish-fulfilling gem that can fulfill others' wishes. It's all up to you and the amount of effort that you are willing to put into your own study and practice.

If you can apply the teachings and practice—not just when you attend retreats or visit a temple but throughout your daily life—then your efforts will not be in vain and you will please the lineage masters and yidam deities. Wealth is something impermanent and will again dissolve into emptiness, so offering money may be of some limited benefit in maintaining a center or supporting your teacher's activities, but the best offering is if you can correctly practice the teachings you have received and attain freedom from samsara. As it is said, "Even if you offer a mansion full of gold or the wealth of the four continents, it will not please your teacher, for it is no better than a heap of donkey's dung. However, if you apply the teachings in practice, that will really please your master." If you properly practice the teachings you have received, you will be freed from samsara, and that is the best way to fulfill the wishes of the buddhas and bodhisattvas.

Intention and Motivation

WE ALREADY POSSESS enlightened mind, buddha nature; it has been there from the very beginning, but we cannot see it because of our obscurations. The only way to see it is to practice the Dharma, confess our negative actions, purify our obscurations, and keep following the right path. If there were no omniscient wisdom within us, there would be no point in going through the hardships of practicing Dharma. For instance, if there is gold in the earth, we can find it by digging, but if there is no gold, then we won't find any no matter how much we dig. Likewise, buddha nature is within us, and we have the potential to awaken it, so it is through digging away obscurations with the shovels of confession and purification that our buddha nature will become apparent.

It is said that Dharma practice depends on our motivation, and if we don't do the prayers for the dedication of merit, our practice won't have much effect. Whatever practice we engage in, such as prostrations, yidam deity practice, mantra recitation, and so forth, our pure motivation is the most important factor for it to be successful, and as soon as we finish our practice, we should dedicate it with prayers. If we don't do dedication prayers for the benefit of all beings, then the merit won't be very vast, and if, due to our self-attachment, we only practice for our own benefit or our family's, the merit won't be very beneficial. For instance, when we have a headache, all we can think is, "How can I get rid of my headache?" When we have stomachache, all we can think is, "How can I get rid of my stomachache?" When we try to earn money, all we can think is, "How can I make more money?" We focus only on our own benefit. But usually all beings have similar needs and desires, so instead of just thinking about our own selfish needs, we should think, "How can all sentient beings be free of suffering?" Instead of just focusing on ourselves, whatever practice we engage in should be done with a vast motivation, not just for ourselves but for all beings. That way the benefits and results will be very vast.

It is also taught that if we practice with devotion and pure perception, we will definitely experience signs, such as good dreams and so forth. But if we do a little practice and get too excited about these things and become attached to them, they turn into obstacles. Therefore, when you get positive signs, you should think it is due to your master's blessings, and when you get negative signs like sickness and so forth, you should understand that it is due to your negative karma, which can be purified through such difficulties. Whatever occurs, good or bad, you should just carry on with your practice without expectation and consider that your pain and discomfort will purify the negative actions of all beings. In that way, your suffering can benefit all beings.

Your intention is the most important thing, and with such an attitude your difficulties can be meaningful. No matter what pain and hardships you face during the practice, you should supplicate the Three Jewels, considering that it is due to the ripening of your negative karma and is purifying your obscurations, and thereby generate a pure motivation. Someone who understands the Dharma can understand that one's own pain and difficulties can eliminate the sufferings of beings, but this is not something you should tell sick and tormented beings who have no idea about Dharma practice—they will just get more upset.

Dharma practice is something that concerns your mind. You can make anything meaningful and beneficial by transforming the way you think. For example, when you have a headache, if you just get depressed about it, your headache will be meaningless and have no benefit whatsoever. Instead you should consider that the pain can be made meaningful with the thought that you are not the only being experiencing a headache, but countless beings in this world experience headaches and much more severe pain and suffering. You should then generate the wish that by your experiencing this headache, the pain and sickness of all beings may ripen. If you think in this way, your headache can become beneficial not only for yourself but for others too.

ANGER

WE WOULD ALL like to attain high realization, but due to the strength of our habituation to disturbing emotions throughout our string of lives, we cannot stop our emotional thoughts. A child doesn't need training in disturbing emotions; at birth children already inherently possess all five poisons. We have spent our entire life involved with mundane activity but still can't give up clinging to it, right? No matter how much trouble we must endure to accomplish worldly affairs, we just tolerate it; no matter how much material wealth we possess, we never think, "Now I have enough"— we still want more. Mind is emptiness, and no matter what may arise from that emptiness, we never feel content.

Due to the power of our afflictions and strong attachment to our present life, the ability to genuinely practice the Dharma is a very rare thing. We need to understand how important it is to practice Dharma and how useful it is to abandon negative acts and practice virtue. Once we get some understanding about this and apply that understanding in our daily life, it will be easier to give up negative actions and generate some diligence and perseverance in the practice of virtuous actions.

Our mind is constantly afflicted by thoughts and emotions; it's like a wild place full of thorny plants, without any good fruit or crops. If we leave our wild mind that way, always afflicted by the five poisons, it will be influenced by them continuously. This will create more and more negative karma, which will keep us wandering through the six realms, and we'll never attain realization and liberation. Obscured by our negative emotions, we have no knowledge about our past or future lives, but if we were even slightly aware of them, we wouldn't relax for even a moment. We would surely not keep carrying on the way we do but would do something about it immediately. But since we can't perceive our past or future lives, we indulge in laziness.

Lord Buddha had a younger half brother called Nanda, who was very passionate and extremely attached to his wife. One day, Nanda invited the Buddha to visit his home. Since the Buddha had no discursive thoughts and no attachment toward his relatives or aversion toward enemies, Nanda was wondering whether the Buddha would actually come. Now the Buddha thought that the time had come to tame Nanda, so he accepted the invitation and went to Nanda's home. Nanda had arranged many offerings to please the Buddha, and the Buddha gave him a lot of teaching. When the Buddha left, Nanda accompanied him to bring the offerings to where the Buddha was residing. Nanda was reluctant to go because he was very attached to his wife and didn't want to be apart from her, so he went to see her before leaving. His wife was also very attached to him and, kissing his forehead, told him to be back before the spot was dry.

After bringing the offerings to the Buddha's residence, Nanda quickly did prostrations and was about to return home, but the Buddha told him to stay and take ordination. As he still longed for his wife, becoming a monk put Nanda in a very difficult situation. He tried to run away many times, but the monks kept catching him and bringing him back to the Buddha.

The only thing Nanda could think about was his wife and nothing else, and as the Buddha knew this, one day he asked Nanda if he wanted to go see the snowy peak of a mountain. Nanda said he did, so the Buddha miraculously transported him to the top of a mountain and told him to have a look around. While looking around at the beautiful scenery spread below, Nanda ran into a one-eyed female monkey, and when the Buddha asked Nanda what he had seen, Nanda said he saw a one-eyed monkey. So Lord Buddha asked, "Which do you find more beautiful, that monkey or your wife?" Nanda replied, "My wife is a hundred, a thousand times more beautiful!"

Then Buddha asked Nanda if he wanted to go see the heavens, and Nanda said that indeed he did. "Good," replied the Buddha, "let's go to the realm of the gods." When they arrived, the Buddha sat down and told Nanda to have a look around. Looking around, Nanda saw how each god lived in his own palace, surrounded by many beautiful young goddesses and enjoying inconceivable pleasure, happiness, and abundance. However, there was one palace with numerous gorgeous goddesses, but no god. When Nanda asked why, he was told, "In the realm of the humans, there is a man called Nanda, a half brother of the Buddha, who is receiving teachings from the Buddha and following the monastic discipline. This action will lead him to be reborn among the gods, and this palace will then be his." Nanda was overjoyed and went back to the Buddha, who asked, "Did you see the young goddesses in the gods' realm?"

"I certainly did!"

"Good. Which do you find more beautiful, your wife or the young goddesses?"

"The daughters of the gods are much more beautiful," replied Nanda. "Indeed, their beauty surpasses even that of my wife Pundarika—as much, in fact, as her beauty surpasses that of the one-eyed monkey we saw on the mountain."

So when they got back to Earth, Nanda observed the monastic discipline perfectly. Then one day the Buddha addressed the monks: "Nanda has renounced worldly life in order to be reborn in the divine realms, but all of you have become monks in order to go beyond suffering. You and he are not on the same path. Do not talk to him anymore, do not be friendly with him, and don't even sit on the same seat with him!" All the monks obeyed, and Nanda got very upset. He thought, "Ananda is my younger brother—at least he will still have some affection and talk to me." But when Nanda went to see his brother, Ananda got up from his seat and moved away. When Nanda asked him why none of the monks would talk to him or even sit near him, Ananda told him what the Buddha had said, and Nanda was heartbroken. In that area there were many monks, but because nobody would talk to him, Nanda became very lonely and so upset that he couldn't eat and grew thin.

At last the Buddha came to see him and said, "Nanda, will you come to see the hells?" Nanda agreed, and the Buddha transported them both there with his miraculous powers and said, "Go and have a look around." So Nanda set off to explore, visiting all the hell realms, and saw the innumerable sufferings of screaming beings who were being tortured, burned in pots, and so forth. In one place, he came across an empty pot with a blazing fire crackling inside it and a large number of the Lord of Death's henchmen all around, so he asked them why there was no one in the pot. "There is a young half brother of the Buddha called Nanda," they replied, "who is practicing the monastic discipline with the intention of being reborn as a god. After enjoying the happiness of the celestial realms, when his merit runs out he will be reborn here." When he heard that, Nanda was terrified and ran away.

Upon his return, he reflected upon all that he had seen and experienced. To be born among the gods in the future and then end up in the hell realms made no sense, so he developed a real determination to seek freedom from samsara. Having seen the hells with his own eyes, he never did the slightest thing to transgress his precepts, and the Buddha extolled him as the disciple with the best control over his senses.

If only we could remember what we have done in our past lives, there is no way we would be as lazy as we are, but since we don't have any foreknowledge, we keep thinking everything is fine and just do whatever we want. But like Nanda, if we don't practice the Dharma properly in this life, we'll just keep getting carried away by our conflicting emotions, never finding happiness or liberation but continuously wandering in the six realms.

Within your emotional mind, all sorts of different thoughts can arise, and you should be certain that though countless disturbing emotions and thoughts may occur, they have no benefit whatsoever and only obscure your path to liberation. All the past great masters totally discarded the eight worldly concerns* and emotional thoughts, and by dedicating their entire life to practice without caring about comfort, they perfected the stages of the path.

In the past, because monkeys can be quite pesky and annoying, practitioners doing retreat in secluded places would often keep one as a pet. They would use their pet monkey in order to train in patience and develop bodhichitta. For us it would be very difficult to have a monkey as a pet, because our five disturbing emotions are so strong that we are constantly getting carried away by them. So instead, whenever any of the five poisons arises, we should try to apply the antidote right there and then.

It's important to keep improving your practice and stabilize it so that it keeps getting better and not worse. Whenever disturbing emotions like anger or desire arise and you give in to them, you should use the Dharma as an antidote. If you don't do so right then, the emotion will become an obstacle. If every time you do a sadhana you repeat the bodhisattva vow but become angry when someone insults you, then you are merely mouthing the words and not applying the vow. For example, someone might say, "I'm really trying my best to practice bodhichitta, but this guy owes me a lot of money and never pays me back, so I get really angry with him; I just cannot generate bodhichitta for him." By acting that way, they break their vow, because no matter how much someone harms you, you still have to generate loving-kindness toward that being. Even if you cannot benefit the person in this life, you should pray to benefit him or her in future lives.

---

* The eight worldly concerns are attachment to gain, pleasure, praise, and fame, and aversion to loss, pain, blame, and bad reputation.

When a certain object becomes the cause of your disturbing emotions, you should develop loving-kindness and consider that object as a support for your Dharma practice. When the antidote works, it is a sign that your Dharma practice is starting to take hold. For instance, in the beginning you may still get angry, but as your mindfulness improves and you keep applying the antidote, it will occur less frequently and not be as intense. You may still get carried away by anger and other emotions, but if you confess immediately and make a commitment not to get overwhelmed by them again, over time they will lessen. As you work with your mind in that way, your practice will gradually improve.

It's very important to keep examining your mind at all times and be aware of what occurs in it. We have this habit of criticizing others; we are very good at pointing out their faults, but we have a hard time being aware of our own flaws. Examining the faults of others will not benefit anyone and only leads to more disturbing emotions, blocking our path to liberation. Whatever anyone else does, let them do it. It's not your business to find other people's flaws, and even if you do point them out, there is no way for you to correct them. On the other hand, it is very important to watch your own mind and train in subduing and reducing your own disturbing emotions. Analyze your mind, constantly watch your thoughts, recognizing whether they are positive or negative, and become aware of your faults. If you constantly observe yourself and analyze your thoughts, you will eventually be able to tame your mind. Since we haven't been able to purify our karmic and emotional obscurations, our gross disturbing emotions can come up anytime, and whenever these emotions come up, we should apply the antidote by looking into our mind and trying to understand that all phenomena are emptiness. If you leave your mind in a relaxed state without contriving anything, disturbing emotions will cease.

Again and again supplicating your master from the bottom of your heart is also of great importance. Especially whenever dualistic thoughts and disturbing emotions arise, pray to your root master, the embodiment of the buddhas of the three times in the form of Guru Padmasambhava; as you rest in that state of supplication, your afflictions will vanish. Again and again, whenever you communicate or talk to others, don't forget your training, but keep examining your mind. Otherwise, whatever you say will be influenced by anger, attachment, or ignorance.

Though in general our disturbing emotions are always present, in particular whenever we have very strong emotions—such as anger when we see someone we can't stand, or lust when we see someone we are attached to, or jealousy when we see someone with great wealth that we covet—we should immediately apply the antidote without following our afflicted thoughts. Although there are many harmful spirits, gods, demons, ghosts, and other negative forces that influence us so that we experience sickness, obstacles, and other difficulties, instead of getting angry at them we should rouse great compassion toward them and rest in that state of compassion. The more we generate compassion and loving-kindness toward anyone who wants to harm us, the less they can affect us, so meditating in that way is very beneficial.

The main cause of birth in the hell realm is anger, which is the most harmful of the five afflicting emotions. When we see a small snail with horns and touch it lightly, it immediately retracts; similarly, our mind instantly gets angry, even when our feelings are only slightly hurt. When someone makes even the slightest remark in a certain manner or looks at us in a certain way, we immediately get angry, or sometimes when we put on some clothes and don't like the way they look on us, we tear them off and throw them on the floor, or when we pour tea in our cup and spill some, we instantly get furious. Even among our friends, with the slightest thing that displeases us, such as a look or remark, we immediately get angry without even noticing it. That's why we always have to keep an eye on our mind, and whatever daily activities we engage in—sitting, walking, eating, or sleeping—we should constantly watch our thoughts. Being mindful and aware of our thoughts and feelings helps to reduce our disturbing emotions.

We shouldn't get angry about meaningless things, as this harms others and causes us to suffer endlessly in samsara. If we don't keep an eye on our mind, all sorts of negative things are bound to happen. In Tibet, there was an ongoing feud between the people of Jarong, a region on the border with China, and the Chinese, which started over nothing more than a piece of bread. First it was just a quarrel about bread, and as each side was defending its own tradition and both sides were supported by their family and friends, it ended up being a huge fight that dragged on for many years. Because of an insignificant quarrel, many people on both sides suffered for twelve years and some lost their lives.

We often will point out someone's faults, saying things like, "That is not the way to behave!" It's very easy to say that about someone else, but we never examine ourselves. It's crucial to see our own mistakes first, for if we recognize and purify our own mistakes, everything else becomes very easy. If we point out someone else's faults by scolding them, they just get angry. Even if we think we're helping them, we're doing more harm than good. As Dharma practitioners, we must reduce disturbing emotions, not increase them.

When we do housework like cleaning and cooking, we even get angry at inanimate objects when things don't work the way we want, and we may not even notice that we're angry. Often there are animate beings experiencing the temporary hells who live for a time inside inanimate objects such as doors, windows, pillars, ropes, brooms, and so forth, and these beings have feelings and experience a lot of suffering. That is why it's important to always maintain a sense of peace and gentleness in body, speech, and mind.

Whatever we do, one way or another we are always afflicted by our emotions. For instance, we instantly get excited when someone tells us how great they think we are, and as soon as we get even the slightest scolding, we instantly burst into a fit of anger. But when we analyze these situations, there really is no reason to get angry or arrogant. Any emotional thought that occurs makes us accumulate negative actions, and no matter what we do in this world, there is never a time when we're not controlled by disturbing emotions. The slightest little thing tends to give rise to disturbing emotions, so it's crucial to try to recognize our thoughts and emotions so that they don't overwhelm us. Especially among family members and friends, it's very important to be extremely patient. If we don't meditate on patience, we may cause a lot of harm to others.

So at all times, please be mindful and aware, analyzing and watching your mind so that you don't get carried away by your disturbing emotions. Whatever Dharma practice you do, it's crucial to give up the eight worldly concerns, because as long as you're involved with them, your Dharma practice will never be successful. Our own mind is obvious to us: we know what we think, so whatever disturbing emotions arise, try to recognize them and get rid of them.

From beginningless lifetimes until now, again and again we have been totally obscured by the five poisons. From one life to the next we have done nothing but follow the disturbing emotions that automatically keep occurring in our mind. When practicing the Dharma, we should reduce our distractions, and if we don't feel faith and respect, we should try to develop it.

You may not perceive a lot of suffering right now, but you should understand the nature of suffering and the rare opportunity to practice Dharma, contemplate it, and integrate it in your mind. Developing one-pointed faith and respect with body, speech, and mind, supplicate your root master, with the determination to take refuge in your master until perfect enlightenment, and pray, "Please bless me with your compassion!" Then let your body, speech, and mind abide in a relaxed state while engaging in the supplication prayers with complete trust in your root guru. Lastly, unless your merit is sealed with dedication prayers, whatever merit you have accumulated for countless aeons may be instantly destroyed by your giving in to a moment of anger—so please be careful in your conduct. When someone makes you angry, you should meditate on compassion and patience and not retaliate when others criticize, hurt, or insult you. Instead, try to control your anger and meditate on compassion toward the person who makes you angry. Besides, if you carefully analyze it, the object of your anger is no other than emptiness anyway.

PRIDE AND EGO-CLINGING

SADLY, SENTIENT BEINGS have a habit of being constantly carried away by afflictive emotions. Even though we don't have many qualities of experience and realization, if we have the slightest experience, we tend to think that we are very special and become arrogant. Both on the spiritual path and on the mundane level, pride is something that blocks our progress and the development of good qualities, so it is very important to be free of pride and not succumb to arrogance.

The fact is that pride is the biggest obstacle to developing qualities such as loving-kindness and compassion, for pride is like an iron ball: no matter how long it's submerged, it will never absorb water. Similarly, if you think you are special, your pride will harden you and thus prevent you from developing more positive inner qualities. Even among fellow practitioners, we often think that we are better than others, but entertaining such thoughts without subduing our pride makes it very difficult to receive the blessings of the Dharma. Unfortunately, most of the time we're not even aware of it, so you must continually observe yourself, examine your faults, and subdue your negative emotions.

If you have property or wealth, you might think, "I'm so rich and special," and if you are good-looking, you might think, "I'm so beautiful and much better than they are." Or if you have a good voice, you might think, "I have such a beautiful voice." But all that just keeps increasing your disturbing emotions. You may have had a good education and developed quite a few mundane qualities, but concerning the sacred Dharma you have no qualities whatsoever, and any knowledge you may have acquired on a worldly level will only lead to the lower realms or keep you wandering in samsara. Since you don't have even the slightest spiritual quality, you should never be proud. No matter what occurs, please stay humble.

It's our emotional thoughts that bind us to samsara, and even though we engage in Dharma practice, we tend to remain attached to dualistic thought. In Tibet, there is a saying: "Whether your head gets hit by a stone or a golden statue, the effect is the same: a fractured skull." Similarly, whether we are proud of our worldly accomplishments or our spiritual accomplishment, the result is the same. What we need to do in all situations is strive to get rid of our ego-clinging. It really all comes down to that: ego-clinging is what keeps us wandering in samsara. However, if we analyze the ego, we'll discover that it doesn't actually exist.

When we say "I," it's something very special to us. When our five disturbing emotions are blazing, whatever worldly conversation is going on, we always think it's something about us. When we practice, we think, "I did well today; I am getting better" or "I have such profound realization." But once we become free from that self-attachment, there is no more trouble. Examining the concept of "I," we'll never find one. Is your body the "I"? When your corpse is cremated, does the "I" die with it? When your breathing stops, does your "I" leave? No, the "I" doesn't die, for it still experiences the bardo after death. Your ego seems to be very concrete and solid, experiencing pain and difficulties, and even without your body you still feel an "I" or cling to it. Please examine what this "I" is—search for it. Wherever you search for it, you won't find any "I." You only have a sense that it exists, and this sense is called "clinging."

When we develop anger and pride, there is no other place to go except the hell realms. Yet, practicing Dharma means taming our afflictive emotions, not increasing them, so there is no need to create a future birth in the hell realms. Instead of feeding your pride, consider all beings the way a mother treats her only child, developing great compassion toward them. If you don't develop bodhichitta, you will find the path to liberation blocked. Of course you have heard all this before, and you may know it intellectually, but that's not enough—you must keep it in mind and train in it continually.

One must be like a yak whose horns are cut off: without horns, a yak becomes very humble, and that's how we should be. Don't get carried away by pride; instead, remain humble and simple. If we have any good qualities, people will respect us, but this respect will not benefit us at all. It just degenerates our own merit. The respect of others increases our arrogance and obstructs our accomplishment of the practice. It increases our negative actions, and there's no benefit to that whatsoever. Of course, when you study Dharma, you must have confidence that you can accomplish your studies, but if you know just a little bit, you might start to think that you are a great scholar, which is something to avoid. Pride and arrogance make it very difficult to accomplish anything on the path. You might think that you know something, but not compared to the Buddha. You don't possess even an atom of the qualities he has.

Take me, for example. I was recognized as a master at a very young age, went through all the traditional trainings, and became the object of refuge for thousands of monks. Through the kindness of my masters, I received all the empowerments, transmissions, and instructions; I even did some practice, but it's very difficult to be able to practice correctly, isn't it? Many people believe that I'm a great master as I'm a reincarnation, and respect me as the object of prostrations, but personally I don't care for all that. It's only because I have some merit that people pay respect and prostrate to me, but that merit will degenerate. Whenever I sit on a throne and people start prostrating, I never feel like I'm someone great or special, but I do feel a great deal of loving-kindness toward all beings and sincerely want to fulfill their wishes, whoever they might be, so I do seem to have developed a little bodhichitta. I have a high level of confidence and a certain amount of power, but I have never developed any pride, and whatever I have done, such as constructing elaborate supports for the representations of enlightened body, speech, and mind in Tibet and India, I did to benefit others, so I have felt happy not for myself but for them.

Because of our karma and disturbing emotions, it will be difficult for the blessings of a yidam deity or lineage master to enter our minds. The self is the cause of all our problems and is very powerful, and until we release our strong clinging to this concept of an "I," we cannot really attain enlightenment. This ego-clinging is very difficult to get rid of, as it is totally integrated into our being, so we should continuously contemplate and focus on getting rid of it.

At the beginning of yidam practices, in which we visualize deities, we often find a verse to dispel obstructors in which we offer them a torma. But the obstructors are really nothing other than our own ego-clinging, and once we get rid of that self-attachment, there is no need to get rid of anything external because it cannot affect us. If we don't get rid of our self-attachment, then there are indeed external negative forces, and the more we cling to the self, the more powerful they become.

It's important to get rid of all arrogance and become humble, noble, and free of pride about your practice and accomplishments. You might have certain experiences and realizations that you would like to tell others about, but there is nothing special about such experiences, and you should keep them to yourself. One of the four maras is the devaputra mara, the demon of the divine child, which refers to pride and distraction. Whether lamas, monks, nuns, or lay practitioners, we are all deceived by pride and distraction. When good thoughts or signs appear, such as rainbows in the sky or visions of deities, we give rise to pride and attachment about them. We may also have good dreams about seeing deities and going to buddha fields, so we feel very joyful and excited, but when practicing the yidam deity and having good experiences and realization, we shouldn't get carried away by pride, thinking, "I have such a good practice!" Since we are worldly people, of course we will have such emotions, but if we get attached to these things, we are still bound—but with golden chains. Instead, we should just keep doing our practice and rest within the nature of awareness, without holding on to these experiences. Otherwise, our practice will not improve and we won't make any progress. Whatever good experience you have, you should develop faith and devotion; then your experience and realization will develop and your good qualities will unfold. The moment you have dualistic concepts of subject and object, that itself is the worst obscuration that blocks good qualities. Whatever thought arises, good or bad, you should be free of doubt and not hold on to it.

Once there were two lamas who encountered two evil spirits, and each of the spirits decided to follow one of the lamas to cause him harm. One spirit immediately killed the lama he was following, but the other spirit helped the lama he was following attain some good signs like clairvoyance and miraculous power, so that lama became very arrogant about having such great qualities and started deceiving many beings, and when he died he was reborn in hell. Later, when the two spirits met again, the first one said that he killed the lama immediately. Hearing this, the other spirit said, "You didn't really cause much harm then." To which the first one replied, "Then what did you do to the lama you were following?" The second spirit explained, "I helped him attain clairvoyance and other magical powers so that he became quite famous. Due to this he became quite arrogant and his disturbing emotions increased, so when he died he was reborn in hell, where he still remains."

We have no real external enemies. Our true enemies are the five disturbing emotions within us: desire, anger, ignorance, jealousy, and pride. It is due to them that we have endlessly wandered in samsara. These five are the result of clinging to our ego. Such ego-clinging causes the worst obscurations and can cast us into the hell realms. If we have outer enemies, we can physically defeat them with the help of weapons, but no weapons will help overcome our inner enemies, the five disturbing emotions: they can only be defeated by our supplicating the Three Jewels and subduing our mind through Dharma practice.

Thus, without following your dualistic thoughts, and with single-pointed devotion, try to focus on your practice. Whatever Dharma practice you do, your awareness should be very stable and one-pointed—that's essential. Since beginningless time, we have done nothing but develop disturbing emotions and generate further attachment to them, so it's very hard to reduce our conceptual thoughts. But, when properly trained, even animals like birds, dogs, and horses can learn and understand; as human beings with a sense of intelligence, we can train and learn how to practice properly without deceiving ourselves, and we can gradually improve. However, if we have a strong sense of ego-clinging, then we cannot practice the Dharma correctly. For instance, if you throw an iron ball in the water, it instantly sinks to the bottom. Similarly, our ego-clinging drags us to the bottom of samsara. But if you hammer out the iron ball until it is flat and then throw it in the water, it will float. Likewise, if you subdue and purify your innate ego-clinging, you can eventually avoid sinking into samsara.

MINDFULNESS

OUR MINDS ARE totally unpredictable, just like plants during the summer rains: all kinds of thoughts, both good and bad, spring up. But following thoughts and creating more concepts is not what Dharma is about. Dharma is about trying to decrease thoughts and subdue our mind. Nonetheless, thoughts do arise constantly, and in worldly life we are so busy that we don't even notice that this process goes on continuously. For instance, most of the time our mind is turned outward, always noticing things we don't like in others and judging other people's actions and speech, but that just increases our own emotions. It has never been taught that we will attain enlightenment by judging others; it is not taught that we need to subdue others' minds but rather to subdue our own mind. Another example is businesspeople who are constantly busy figuring out how to increase profits by buying this and selling that, yet they aren't even aware that such thoughts are constantly running through their minds. There is not even an instant when we are free of these ceaseless thoughts and emotions—that's the character of sentient beings. Without analyzing your mind, you won't have a clue how many thoughts occur in it, but once you start examining it, the constant stream of thoughts feels like a storm and you might not be able to relax even for an instant. Most of our thoughts concern the five disturbing emotions. Whether it's a very strong emotion or not, and whether we accumulate karma or not, once a thought has occurred, mental karma is accomplished. When we follow a thought and carry it out physically and verbally, we create strong negative karma.

For beginningless lifetimes, we have been ruled by our disturbing emotions, so the five poisons are very strongly present in our minds. Always caught up in our ego, we are incredibly proud, thinking, "I'm so great, so beautiful, so special," yet if we really think about it, we might have a few minor qualities, but they don't amount to very much. And even though we think we are so healthy and beautiful, if we analyze our body it's nothing but a bag of skin filled with blood, pus, shit, urine, and so on—the thirty-six disgusting substances. We care for our body so well and try to look very beautiful, putting on makeup and so forth, but that's all based on the afflictive emotion of pride. Likewise, if we examine our mind, we see that it's nothing but deluded thoughts based on the five poisons that constantly arise. So what's the point of thinking we are so great, beautiful, or special?

In many countries, including the United States, people often think they are very powerful. But if we examine whether we have any power, we'll discover that we really don't have that much. In this life we can't even accomplish the activities we've planned, and when we die, we have no idea where we'll go and have no power over where we end up—it all depends on our karma. When our terminal illness has arrived, the Lord of Death ties a big rope around our neck and drags our corpse away. There is nothing we can do about it. Because of our own negative actions, we'll experience the punishment accordingly. Even though we may cry out for our parents, relatives, and friends to help, and though they may wish to protect us, there is nothing they can do.

So always try to check your own mind and gradually decrease your negative thoughts and emotions. If you keep checking your mind and understand the faults of being angry and proud, you can gradually decrease and subdue your negative emotions. It's not as easy as chopping down a tree, but if you keep examining your mind again and again, your disturbing emotions will gradually subside.

As a Dharma practitioner, it is especially important that you check your mind again and again and try to tame it. If you keep getting carried away with thoughts and emotions, you'll fall back into samsara again and again for countless lifetimes. It's like the story of the lama who was quite wealthy and then got robbed of all his possessions by a gang of bandits. After that, realizing the futility of wealth, he decided to give up worldly life and started practicing in a secluded place. He used to make water offerings in which he put some grains of barley, and after making the offering he would put it outside, so many pigeons came to feed on it. Seeing how many pigeons he could gather there to eat the grains, he began to think that if he could gather a similar number of people, he could take revenge on those who stole from him. As he became caught up in these thoughts, his emotions kept increasing. Eventually, he got so carried away that he ended up leaving his retreat and started putting together his own gang in order to get even with the bandits. So you should maintain constant vigilance and keep checking your mind again and again. When you do have positive thoughts like devotion and faith, you should rejoice and consider it to be due to your master's blessing. No doubt it is difficult to control your afflicted mind, but the more you train, the easier it gets. Don't exert yourself for a short time and then give up if there is no immediate result; instead, your efforts should be steady and continuous.

Enlightenment occurs only when your disturbing emotions are completely exhausted. Turning your mind inward, watch your thoughts and analyze whether they are positive or negative. If you have negative thoughts or disturbing emotions, get rid of them like poison, and if you have even an instant of virtuous thought, try to increase it. Developing faith, devotion, and a steady confidence in the Three Jewels, engage in your prayers. You should chant the supplication prayers from the depths of your heart, and whenever virtuous or unvirtuous thoughts arise, don't follow or get carried away by them, but focus on praying to your master and mingling your mind with your master's. Repeatedly supplicating your master, the embodiment of all the buddhas and bodhisattvas of the three times; receiving the four empowerments; mingling your mind with the enlightened mind of your master; and resting in that nature is the way to receive blessings and make progress.

These days there are many people who have practiced for some time and think they have perfected the practice and attained enlightenment, but whether you have attained enlightenment can be seen merely by examining your own mind and checking whether your disturbing emotions and dualistic thoughts have been purified and exhausted. There is no need to ask anyone else—just analyze your own mind and you'll find out. If you discover that your disturbing emotions and dualistic thoughts have been exhausted, omniscient wisdom has arisen, and if bodhichitta spontaneously arises and remains inseparable from your being, that's quite a good sign. Honestly check your own mind to see how much pride, anger, and desire you have, and you'll know immediately where you are in your practice.

In Tibet, people who are rich often wear very simple clothes, and people who are poor wear rather fancy clothes in an effort to show off. Similarly, Dharma practitioners who have profound experiences and realization will never talk about it, but those without experience or realization like to show off their practice, which then disrupts their accumulation of merit. If you have accumulated one hundred thousand Avalokiteshvara mantras, going around telling everybody will only decrease the merit.

When you get up in the morning, pray to your teacher and promise not to let your mind get carried away with unvirtuous thoughts and disturbing emotions, and perform as many virtuous actions as possible throughout the day. When you're about to go to sleep, don't just plop down on your bed but check what you have done that day. Calculate how many negative things you did and how many virtuous actions you performed, and when you find that you practiced well and did something virtuous, rejoice in it. If you didn't practice Dharma and just committed negative acts, take stock of such faults. Tell yourself that you still have no control over your mind and that you have created negative karma since beginningless time, doing the same thing over and over again. Then, before your guru and all the buddhas and bodhisattvas of the three times, promise to not do it again. Always train in mindfulness, alertness, and carefulness, the three qualities that guard your mind and conduct. With mindfulness you can concentrate on what to adopt and what to reject, with alertness you can check if you act according to the Dharma or not, and with carefulness you can watch and train your body, speech, and mind in accordance with the Dharma. Your body should be humble and calm, seated in the proper posture when you practice; your speech should avoid harmful words, lies, and slander, speaking in a gentle way in harmony with others; and your mind should always be kind.

Someone who practices pure Dharma will not wander in the lower realms. I have never heard of a pure Dharma practitioner who ended up wandering in the lower realms; it never happened before and it won't happen in the future. All activities that you engage in, both worldly activities and Dharma activities, primarily depend on your mind. When you do things with a clear mind and supplicate your master in the form of Padmasambhava, you can receive his blessings. You shouldn't have wrong views, doubts, or uncertainties, but have a single-pointed mind. Whatever worldly or Dharma activities you engage in, stability is the most important thing. Worldly people have many different concepts, wondering whether they should do this or that or not. Before starting any worldly activity, we should check thoroughly whether it will have a positive outcome and whether we'll be able to accomplish it. Otherwise, we may go through all sorts of hardship and experience nothing but trouble, without any positive outcome. So you should always first check what the benefit of the action will be and whether you have the capacity to accomplish it; then, if you figure that you do, you should go ahead with it. The same goes for Dharma practice: you should start out by analyzing and checking if you can accomplish it, and once you have chosen a master and a practice and decided to pursue it, it is important to stick to it. It's no good to keep jumping from one teacher or practice to another.

Padmasambhava

THERE ARE COUNTLESS different religions in this world, but foremost among them are the extraordinary teachings of the omniscient Buddha Shakyamuni. The Buddhadharma is based on great compassion for all beings, not on pride, a desire for fame, or any of the disturbing emotions. The chance to study and practice these teachings is due to great merit, so it should not be squandered.

Upon attaining perfect enlightenment in Bodhgaya, Buddha Shakyamuni thought, "I attained perfect realization of the absolute nature of phenomena, profound and vast, but since nobody will be able to understand it, it's useless to teach." Nevertheless, both Indra, who is the king of the gods, and Brahma presented him with vast offerings of white conch shells turning clockwise, golden Dharma wheels, and so on, beseeching him to teach. Thus he gave the first Dharma teachings, turning the Dharma wheel of the four noble truths in Sarnath for his five original disciples. The four truths are the truth of suffering, the truth of the cause of suffering, the truth of cessation, and the truth of the path.

During the Buddha's time, there were often debates and discourses between scholars of different religions arguing which tradition was true. Hinduism and Buddhism both being very profound, two brothers, who were great Brahmin scholars, were unable to decide which teaching to follow. They tended to debate and argue a lot, leading their mother to scold them, "Why are you always arguing? If you really want to know the truth, go to Mount Kailash, for there you will come to understand everything." So they went to Mount Kailash, where they came upon the goddess Umadevi plucking flowers in a meadow. They asked her why she was picking flowers, and she replied that the Buddha had been invited there and was expected to arrive the next day, so she wanted to make him a flower offering. The two scholars decided to join her to meet the Buddha and his retinue. The next day, they made offerings to the Buddha and received teachings, and thereby they gained confidence in the Buddhadharma. In fact, each of the brothers wrote a book delineating the differences between Hinduism and Buddhism. They explained that perfect enlightenment depends on realizing the true nature, and thus they praised the Buddhist teachings as superior.

The buddhas in nirmanakaya form usually teach just the Vinaya, the Sutras, and the Abhidharma but not Secret Mantra. When the buddhas teach Secret Mantra, they appear in sambhogakaya form, and the teachings of the Great Perfection originate from the dharmakaya buddha. So, for ordinary disciples, Buddha Shakyamuni mainly taught the Tripitaka: the three baskets of the Sutras, Vinaya, and Abhidharma. However, in the form of a heruka, he also taught the Secret Mantra and the Great Perfection to a few special disciples. For example, Shakyamuni gave King Indrabhuti teachings on the law of cause and effect and interdependent origination, and he told the king about undergoing severe hardships. But the king, who was very powerful and always surrounded by immense wealth and many queens, told the Buddha, "I don't mind if I'm born as a wolf in the forest—I don't want to give up all my comfort and wealth in order to practice Dharma." Through his omniscience, the Buddha knew it was time for the king to encounter the Secret Mantrayana, so he instantly manifested the mandala of the eight glorious herukas and gave him all the empowerments. As soon as the empowerments were finished, King Indrabhuti attained complete realization and accomplished the bhumis and paths. His realization and liberation were simultaneous due to the perfect circumstance in which the compassionate blessings of the Buddha met with the king's faith, devotion, and pure karma.

Several decades after Buddha Shakyamuni passed into parinirvana, hundreds of thousands of dakinis supplicated Padmasambhava with the same seven-line prayer that we chant to this day. Due to this, he took miraculous birth from a lotus flower in Oddiyana to the northwest of India and taught the Great Perfection teachings to innumerable dakinis. And in order to turn the Dharma wheel of the Secret Mantra for the sake of liberating all beings, the past, present, and future buddhas all blessed Padmasambhava.

Padmasambhava is not just a historical figure who lived in India and then went to Tibet. He didn't appear only in the Saha world during this aeon but attained enlightenment countless aeons ago. Though in reality he was completely enlightened from the very beginning, to sentient beings it appeared as though he relied on many teachers, receiving transmissions from the dharmakaya buddha Samantabhadra up to his own root teacher, doing the practices and attaining realization and accomplishment. He did so for the sake of showing beings the correct way of receiving teachings from an unbroken lineage of teachers and how to follow such teachings in order to receive the lineage blessings.

Just by supplicating Padmasambhava with the seven-line prayer, we can be born in the pure lands, and by reciting this prayer without doubt or hesitation, we can be freed from any unwanted conditions and accomplish whatever we want, including the peaceful, increasing, magnetizing, and wrathful activities and even gain whatever material wealth we desire.

Even though he was primordially enlightened, because the teachings need to be transmitted from master to disciple for the sake of preserving the lineage, Padmasambhava lived in the eight sacred cemeteries in India, where he received teachings from eight mahasiddhas who displayed miracles in these sacred places. These eight vidyadharas also received these teachings through transmission from master to disciple and showed their accomplishment through miracles. It is not that Padmasambhava didn't have knowledge of the teachings he received from these great masters, but in order to preserve the Dharma lineage in an authentic way, he had to receive them again. We too should receive transmissions from a qualified teacher and practice them without any breaches of samaya.

Before coming to Tibet, Padmasambhava had already lived in India for more than two thousand years, and during that time he did nothing but benefit beings in different manifestations through various activities and in various forms. For instance, at the glorious Nalanda University, there were tens of thousands of great scholars. This university had four main gates that were guarded by the greatest scholars, who were also highly realized. Once it happened that five hundred Hindu scholars came to Nalanda and demanded a debate with the scholars. It was decided that everyone had to follow the religion of the winner of the debate. The Hindu scholars were very learned and also had great miraculous powers. The Buddhist scholars at Nalanda were confident that they could win the debate but worried that the Hindus might be better at performing miracles, which would cause a great problem. One night, they all had the same dream about a dakini who said that the Buddhist scholars in fact wouldn't be able to match the Hindu scholars in miracles and should invite her brother from Cool Grove charnel ground to help, or they would lose the debate. The scholars said they were too scared to travel to the charnel ground, so how could they invite him? So the dakini told them that they didn't need to actually go there: she would invite him, and all they had to do was prepare an elaborate ganachakra feast offering and chant the seven-line prayer to invoke him. So the scholars prepared an extensive feast offering according to the dakini's instructions and started chanting the seven-line prayer with great devotion. After a while, Padmasambhava actually appeared and asked why they had requested his presence. They explained the situation in regard to the upcoming debate and their concerns about not being able to match the Hindus' miraculous performances. When the debates started, the Hindu scholars showed amazing miracles such as flying in the sky, but Padmasambhava showed much greater and faster miracles, so the Hindu scholars lost the debate and had to convert to Buddhism.

Based on aspirations during many lifetimes, Padmasambhava came and brought Buddhism to Tibet. If he had not been invited to Tibet, Buddhism couldn't have spread there because of the very powerful local gods and spirits. But Padmasambhava subdued them all, conferred empowerment on them, taught them the Dharma, and bound them by oath so that they all became protectors of the Dharma rather than enemies. Among the local deities and spirits in Tibet, many performed miracles and challenged Padmasambhava, and the places where this occurred can still be visited today.

Evil government officials also challenged Padmasambhava in many ways, but they couldn't prevent him from establishing the Dharma or teaching Secret Mantra. The fact that the Buddha's teachings flourished in Tibet is due to Padmasambhava's blessings. He also caused other great panditas and translators to come to Tibet to spread the Dharma; he gradually gave the bodhisattva vows as well, so that others also started working for the flourishing of the Dharma.

During King Trisong Deutsen's reign, the king and ministers invited Padmasambhava to build Samye Monastery, and when everything was complete and the consecration of the temple and the images was concluded, the king requested Padmasambhava to teach the Dharma. So Padmasambhava went to Samye Chimphu, followed by the king and his subjects. As the foundation of all Secret Mantra teachings is the empowerment, he started by giving the empowerments for the eight herukas and disclosing the mandala. Padmasambhava then asked his disciples whom they wanted to receive the empowerment from: himself or the yidam deity? As everyone could clearly perceive the mandala of the eight herukas, most of them said that since the yidam deity is inseparable from the master, they wanted to receive it from the master. But King Trisong Deutsen's wife, Queen Margyenma, said that since they could always see the master but never saw the deity, she wanted to receive empowerment from the deity. At the beginning of a sadhana, we always project light rays emanating from our heart that invoke the mandala deities in front of us, right? So when Guru Padmasambhava did that, everyone could see the entire mandala, but when the deities dissolve into oneself as one says *Ja Hung Bam Ho*, as the Eight Heruka mandala deities dissolved into Padmasambhava's heart, the queen didn't receive the empowerment.

All the twenty-five disciples, however, received the empowerment according to the deity they were connected to through karma and prayers, and they went off to practice in their individual retreats. Through Guru Padmasambhava's blessings and their own good fortune, they each attained accomplishment and showed miraculous signs. When you see a thangka of the twenty-five disciples, it shows all these accomplishments. For example, Khyechung Lotsa could catch birds just by raising his hand in the sky, Mathok Rinchen could eat rock as if it were food, Yaki Wangchuk could instantly gather wild yaks, and Öden Palgyi Wangchuk could reverse the flow of a river. But Queen Margyenma had the wrong view, so she couldn't accomplish anything because of her doubts about the master. That's why we should practice the Dharma not only with the right view and an unwavering mind but with great faith and devotion as well.

After Padmasambhava had completed Samye Monastery, although the king, queens, ministers, and subjects all insisted he stay in Tibet, he said that the time had come to subdue the rakshasas, the cannibal demons, and if he didn't go they would create problems for this world. Since there was nothing more they could do, the king, ministers, and subjects escorted him to the Gungtang Pass. While they gathered there, countless dakinis came with a horse to escort Padmasambhava, and as he mounted the horse and was about to fly into space with the dakinis, he gave them a lot of advice, saying, "If you sincerely supplicate me, I'm always there next to your pillow, inseparable from you all." He promised that he would appear in front of whomever supplicated him and would return to Tibet on the tenth day of every month according to the Tibetan lunar calendar.

All the Secret Mantra and Great Perfection teachings that were given by Padmasambhava to his twenty-five main disciples were written down by his consort Yeshe Tsogyal. Then, through his miraculous powers, these teachings were hidden throughout Tibet. These termas were later revealed by 108 major and minor treasure revealers, and the beings who attained accomplishment and became vidyadharas through these practices are equal to the number of stars in space. All of these practitioners had full confidence in the instructions—not one of them harbored doubts about them. Of course, when you receive the instructions from your master, it's necessary to understand them, but once you've understood them and they have become clear, having even the slightest doubt about those instructions will obstruct your accomplishment for many aeons.

Padmasambhava also left prophetic instructions to perform different ceremonies for protecting Tibet at the time when the Chinese would invade. When Jamyang Khyentse Chökyi Lodrö arrived in Lhasa, he told the Tibetan government that if they built a three-story-high Padmasambhava statue in the form of Nangsi Zilnön, the Glorious Subjugator of Appearance and Existence, there would be no trouble in Tibet for sixty years. Later, however, when Jamyang Khyentse Chökyi Lodrö was staying in Sikkim, the Tibetan government told him that they had not been able to build a three-story-high Nangsi Zilnön statue and had built a ten-foot Guru Dewa Chenpo statue instead and asked if there was anything else they should do. Hearing this, Jamyang Khyentse Chökyi Lodrö told them, "You didn't do what I advised you to, so now there is nothing more that I can do. Making a Guru Dewa Chenpo statue according to the Indian tradition indicates that Tibetans may be able to go to India." He became very sad, covered his head with his robe, and started crying. If they had built that statue according to his command, the Dharma would have flourished in Tibet for another sixty years. Unfortunately, because of their doubts from not understanding the power of Padmasambhava's vast and compassionate blessings and not having enough confidence in Jamyang Khyentse Chökyi Lodrö's words, things took a tragic turn.

According to our ordinary perception, Padmasambhava was born and spent time in India and Tibet, but in fact he is completely beyond birth and death. His enlightened body is unchangeable; only in the eyes of sentient beings does he seem to take birth and pass away at certain times, for in fact he is always present. During each aeon, no matter how many buddhas appear, if there are suitable students for the Secret Mantra teachings, Padmasambhava will manifest and teach the doctrine of Secret Mantra.

I heard that some people in Taiwan have displayed relics that they claimed to be from Guru Padmasambhava, but I don't think that's true, because in fact he never passed away. When Padmasambhava left Tibet, he did so in the presence of the king, queen, ministers, and a vast number of subjects, who came to wish him farewell at the Gungtang Pass. He just flew from there to the Copper-Colored Mountain, so it's not as though he departed in secret.

Some of Padmasambhava's clothes still exist, and his hair was revealed as a treasure in the form of shining, five-colored strands of hair. Until the appearance of Buddha Maitreya and the rest of the thousand buddhas who will appear in this world, Padmasambhava will manifest to benefit beings. It is said that Padmasambhava has eight manifestations and forty submanifestations, and in each world of the billionfold universe he manifested emanations.

Padmasambhava is inseparable from anyone who has sincere devotion to him. Even though during this degenerate time negative beings try to suppress him, since he has a wisdom body and attained the great transformation rainbow body, he is completely beyond being suppressed or not suppressed, so those people only accumulate negative karma and obstruct their own path of liberation.

The Secret Mantra teachings and especially the Great Perfection, or Dzogchen, through which enlightenment can be attained in the great transformation rainbow body within one lifetime, are due to the blessings of Padmasambhava's rainbow body. According to the view of the Secret Mantra, all beings and phenomena are completely perfect from the very beginning, and these teachings were not contrived by ordinary people but established by the dharmakaya buddha Samantabhadra and the three lineages: the mind lineage of the conquerors, the symbolic lineage of the vidyadharas, and the hearing lineage of ordinary beings. The enlightened masters who then transmitted these teachings were completely free of conceptual thoughts about whether they were good or bad, inspiring or not, and didn't contrive anything.

THE VAST AND PROFOUND VEHICLES

THERE IS NO way to attain enlightenment on one's own. Such a thing has never happened in infinite aeons. Shravakas and pratyekabuddhas who appear when a buddha is not manifest in this world can realize the twelve branches of interdependent origination and attain arhatship. They aren't, however, able to attain complete enlightenment and cannot benefit beings in a vast way; they can only liberate themselves from the sufferings of cyclic existence, and their realization is far from complete enlightenment.

In the Sutrayana, one studies and analyzes the teachings and texts, but no matter how extensive the teachings are, they are all based on the essential nature. The Buddha provided many different levels of teaching, which can be categorized into provisional and definitive meaning. These teachings can be studied, analyzed, and examined, but they're not so easy to understand. For instance, when great scholars, such as khenpos, give detailed Sutrayana teachings, the students listen, reflect on, and analyze the teachings and debate on them. They rely on the texts that they have been taught.

In Tibet, there were innumerable great scholars and bodhisattvas, but unless a scholar was told by his root guru to compose a commentary on a specific text or received a prediction from his yidam deity, he would not write one. Even when great scholars or bodhisattvas did write something, they would first check themselves to make sure that their intention was not merely to win respect, prove themselves to be a great scholar, gain material wealth, or acquire a good reputation. As every Dharma text is meant to benefit beings and guide them on the spiritual path, they would only write if they had a pure, unselfish motivation.

Even in the context of the Sutrayana path, though the past great scholars and realized beings wrote many commentaries on the Buddha's teachings, these writings would first be examined by other great scholars to determine whether the text was in exact accord with the Buddha's teachings. If the text did agree with the Buddha's teachings, it would be presented to the Dharma king and discussed with him. If they all agreed that the text was qualified, the writer would be invited to discuss the text and answer questions from the Dharma king and the scholars. If it was perfect and qualified as a text that could benefit beings, the author would be recognized as a good scholar and the text would be respected. If the author claimed to be a scholar but wrote a commentary that the others found not to be in accordance with the Buddha's teachings and therefore not beneficial, they would proclaim that the text had no value. It would then be tied to a dog's tail, and after the dog had run around with it for a while, the text would be thrown into a fire. This was because a commentary would be read by many people, and if it was not in accordance with the teachings of the Buddha, readers could develop wrong views, create negative karma, and fall into the lower realms in their next life.

In the context of the Secret Mantra, unless someone had a certain level of experience or realization, nobody would even think of writing a commentary, even if requested. In the rare event that they did compose something, they would write it exactly according to the words of the lineage transmission, without adding or omitting anything, and would never contrive or change the meaning or the words based on their own thoughts. Nobody would dare to mix in their own ideas, because there are hundreds of thousands of dakinis that hold the Secret Mantra teachings, and when they know that something has been miswritten or contrived, they will cause obstacles.

From the very beginning, the dharmakaya buddha Samantabhadra, the five buddhas, and so forth, gradually transmitted the Secret Mantra teachings that were put in the care of the dakinis, to preserve them without impairment.

Since the teachings of the Great Perfection appeared in this world, countless beings attained accomplishment through these pith instructions, such as the vidyadhara Garab Dorje, who attained the rainbow body along with his retinue of seven hundred thousand disciples. Also his student, the great master Manjushrimitra, accomplished the rainbow body along with three hundred thousand of his disciples. And Shri Singha attained the rainbow body along with several hundred thousand of his disciples.

The Secret Mantrayana teachings explain that all phenomena are primordially pure and that we should train in developing pure vision toward the place where we are, the time, the teacher, the disciples, and the teachings. Usually we see the place where we live as composed of earth and stones and perceive all phenomena in this world as impure. But actually this world is the pure land of Buddha Shakyamuni, and all the buddhas and bodhisattvas perceive it as made of precious stones, jewels, and so forth—totally pure, not at all as we see it. Due to this degenerate time and our impure thoughts, we only see things as impure, but in fact all phenomena are actually completely pure from the very beginning.

According to the Sutrayana, having doubts about the teachings is regarded as a fault, but it's not as grave a fault as in the Secret Mantra, because the Secret Mantra is the heart essence of the Buddha's teachings, so there's no need to have any doubt about it. Having doubts and hesitating will only cause a lot of obstacles for you on the path. There is nothing wrong with analyzing the teachings, but they've already been analyzed by the omniscient enlightened Buddha. A buddha knows the countless lifetimes of every single being down to the most minute detail. If a buddha with such omniscient power and knowledge has already validated these teachings, it's a joke for people like us, with no ability or knowledge, who don't have the slightest clue what will happen tomorrow, to think that we can honestly judge such teachings. What knowledge or wisdom do we have to appraise these teachings? Of course we can analyze and examine them, but since we are constantly carried away by our conceptual thoughts, instead of spending half our lives trying to appraise them, wouldn't it be better to just put them into practice?

THE GREAT PERFECTION

WITHIN BUDDHISM THERE are nine flawless vehicles, each with its own path to liberation. Each vehicle is more powerful than the previous one, and Dzogchen, the Great Perfection, is the summit. All the Buddhist teachings are extremely profound and special, but among them the teachings of the Great Perfection are the most extraordinary.

The Buddha turned the three Dharma wheels of the gradual path and the twelve branches of teachings solely so that others might realize the natural state. According to the Vinaya, in the *Stainless Sutra* the sole purpose of accumulating merit and purifying obscurations for countless aeons is to realize the natural state of the Great Perfection. Also, engaging in kriya, upa, and yoga tantra for three, seven, or sixteen lifetimes is all for the purpose of realizing the natural state. And, of course, the nine vehicles and 6,400,000 teachings of the Secret Mantra Vajrayana, too, have no other purpose.

No matter how much we study the extensive teachings of the higher and lower vehicles, understanding them depends on our own understanding of the Great Perfection, and it's very difficult to come to a definitive understanding of the entire meaning of the Great Perfection at present. Even if you memorize all the teachings of the Buddha, if you don't realize the meaning of the Great Perfection, you won't be able to attain enlightenment. The essence of all the Buddha's teachings is condensed in the Great Perfection, and, as I have said, in order to realize the natural state of the Great Perfection, you need to supplicate your root guru in the form of Padmasambhava, considering him to be the embodiment of all the buddhas of the three times. If through your devotion you can totally connect to your guru's compassion, you can realize the meaning of the natural state.

If you have the capacity, if you practice the teachings of the Great Perfection, they have the potential to bring enlightenment within three, six, or nine years or at least within a single lifetime. But due to our karmic obscurations accumulated since beginningless time, we get carried away by the negative emotions that prevent us from practicing the Dharma correctly. Not being aware of our own faults, if we cannot accomplish the practice immediately, we think it's the fault of the Dharma; we don't realize that it's actually due to our own flaws, and therefore we think that the teachings don't have such potential.

In the noble land of India as well as in Tibet, countless accomplished practitioners attained perfect enlightenment, and hundreds of thousands of practitioners attained the body of rainbow light, either individually or in a group, through the practice of the Great Perfection.

In the Palyul lineage, there is a prediction that one hundred million masters will attain the highest realization. During the life of Rigdzin Kunzang Sherab, Lhundrub Gyaltsen, and Drubwang Pema Norbu, within the Palyul lineage many ordained practitioners had very high realization and completely pure moral conduct, without even the slightest flaw in their vows. When Situ Chöjung was invited to Dhako, my place in eastern Tibet, many yogis and retreatants came running like deer in the forest to see him in order to offer their experiences and realization. After seeing them, he said that most of them were bodhisattvas who had attained one of the bhumis. When Paltrul Rinpoche was staying at Dzachukha, he kept seeing white or rainbow light to the east and asked what monasteries were in that direction. He was told that the most important monastery was Kathok Dorje Den, so he decided to visit Kathok Monastery, which was about a ten-day walk. When he got there, he still saw rainbow light in the east, so he said it didn't come from Kathok. When he asked which monasteries were beyond Kathok, he was told that the light came from Palyul Monastery.

For the sake of the Dharma, we should be able to endure whatever hardships and obstacles we encounter and not give up when we meet with such conditions. Any obstacles that occur on the path will purify karmic obscurations, so if we reflect properly, these conditions are a good sign. We will experience illness and obstacles even if we don't practice the Dharma, but I'm doubtful that they would purify any karmic obscurations. When we practice Dharma and reflect properly, dedicating our merit for the sake of all parent sentient beings, we can accumulate a great deal of merit and purify a lot of karmic obscurations. There are many Dzogchen practitioners who engage in the practice for many months and years and face a lot of illness and hardship, but this purifies obscurations from beginningless lifetimes so that in the future they can move to happier states as explained in the Dzogchen texts.

Even though this degenerate time is one in which the blessings of the sacred Dharma are diminishing, the Dzogchen teachings will flourish from when the average life span is sixty years until it has been reduced to only ten years. Many Dzogchen tantras explain that it is easy to purify obscurations and attain realization through the practice of Dzogchen, so our greatest responsibility is to steadily engage in Dzogchen practice.

PART TWO

THE THREE JEWELS

NEVER FORGET YOUR object of refuge: the precious Three Jewels of Buddha, Dharma, and Sangha. Whenever you encounter problems or trouble, think, "It is up to the Three Jewels!" If you can do that, then even if you have scary dreams, you will instantly remember the Three Jewels in your sleep and they'll console you. Also, if you do this throughout your life, then even if you're not liberated immediately, you'll remember the Three Jewels in the bardo after death and they'll protect you.

The compassion of the buddhas and bodhisattvas in the ten directions is like that of a mother for her only child and is equal for all beings without partiality, but if we cannot connect with them in the proper way, we cannot receive the benefit. This depends on the karmic connection of beings, as well as dependent origination, and without any connection it's difficult to attain liberation. It's not that the Three Jewels don't have enough blessings and compassion, but, lacking faith, devotion, and pure perception, we are not open to these. For instance, if you go fishing and cast your line into the water, if there are fish in the water you'll be able to catch some, but if there aren't any, then you won't get any no matter how many times you cast your line. Similarly, if you lack devotion, then when your master casts his hook of blessing and compassion, he will not be able to catch you to pull you from the ocean of samsara.

If sentient beings could connect with the blessings and compassion of the Three Jewels, they would be led on the path to liberation and no one would be left in samsara, but beings are bound by their karma. The Three Jewels can't just toss us from samsara into enlightenment like throwing a stone. Attaining enlightenment depends on our karma, which is why the Buddha stressed the importance of understanding cause and effect. The Buddha did not teach just because he was a great scholar; he taught with limitless loving-kindness and compassion to make a connection with beings in order to lead them on the path to enlightenment. The sole purpose of the Dharma is to purify the karmic obscurations of beings and lead them to liberation.

In regard to the Sangha, we are very fortunate to be able to gather together to receive teachings and practice, because when we pray together as an assembly, the prayers are much more effective. For instance, when a group of a hundred people kill an animal and enjoy the meat together, all those hundred people will bear the same karmic result arising from killing the animal. The same goes for warfare: the karmic result of killing the enemy extends to the entire army. The karma isn't divided up and shared among them so that each is relieved of some of the karma and just bears a small amount of responsibility, but rather each soldier bears the full result of killing each and every person. This also applies to virtuous actions: When we do prayers together, each one of us accrues the merit. For example, when we accumulate one million *mani* mantras,* each practitioner gets the same amount of merit.

We always think that we're so special and put ourselves above others, but thinking that way has caused us to wander in samsara until now. We long to accomplish something beneficial for ourselves, but we simply aren't able to. In this world there are many very powerful beings, including local deities, spirits, and nagas, who have great power and have lived for many aeons, but even though they have a lot of power, they are still wandering in samsara like the rest of us. The only one who can truly liberate us from samsara is our root guru, who is the very embodiment of the Three Jewels.

All phenomena are emptiness, but they are also inseparable from interdependent arising, and, due to the law of cause and effect, whatever virtuous or negative actions you commit will ripen. So instead of disturbing your mind by worrying all the time, just pray to the Three Jewels. Whenever you experience fear or feel threatened, immediately remember the Three Jewels. If during the day you constantly think that the Three Jewels watch over you, then, as I mentioned earlier, even when you have scary dreams you'll be aware of the Three Jewels protecting you. Remembering the Three Jewels in stressful situations also helps to release mental tension. Even if you are attacked by harmful spirits and feel frightened or your mind becomes unstable, praying to the Three Jewels will have great benefit.

But always remember that whether you are practicing on your own or with others, it is crucial to focus on the supplication prayers from the

---

* *Om mani padma hum* (the mantra of Avalokiteshvara, the deity of compassion).

depths of your heart, without being interrupted by any other thoughts. In this world there is nothing more precious and essential than the Three Jewels, and by depending on them we can part from the sufferings of samsara. Remind yourself of that again and again and never forget it. We cannot immediately see the power of the Three Jewels, but by relying on them we can gradually get rid of our disturbing emotions and ego-clinging. Having planted the seed through their blessings, we can attain the state of liberation and omniscience, which is ultimate peace, bliss, and happiness.

ACCUMULATING MERIT

WE EACH HAVE a wish-fulfilling gem within our mind: our buddha nature. It is much more precious than actual, material gems, which may fulfill our wishes for this life but cannot protect us from suffering in future lives. We don't need to buy or search for this gem—we've always had it. And if we don't realize the qualities of our buddha nature, then no matter how much we endeavor to accumulate merit and purify our obscurations, it will not be of much benefit. It would be like trying to mine gold where there is none. So first you must know where the gold is located; then, if you put forth the effort and persevere in digging there, you will acquire great wealth.

Once you have purified your karmic obscurations and accumulated merit, the qualities of your inner buddha nature, your wish-fulfilling gem, will become manifest. These qualities don't arise from elsewhere but have been within your mind since beginningless time. Buddhas and bodhisattvas who benefit beings have many levels of activity, and though there's no difference between the enlightened qualities of the buddhas, the extent of their activity depends on the intention that they generated in the very beginning. The two accumulations known as the conceptual accumulation of merit and the nonconceptual accumulation of wisdom, no matter how small or big, are always of paramount importance.

Due to the kindness and blessings of Guru Padmasambhava as well as the good karma of the Tibetan people, many treasure revealers manifested in Tibet. Many of these treasure revealers, such as Guru Chöwang, Ratna Lingpa, Nuden Dorje, and others, were extremely powerful. They revealed countless precious Dharma texts, but also many special objects such as vajras, daggers, statues, and so forth, all of which had inconceivable qualities. The great treasure revealer Nuden Dorje was able to reveal whatever objects he needed, such as vajras and bells, musical instruments, carpets, different paints, horses' hooves, colorful banners for temples, and many other substances. This was all due to the power of his merit from past lives. There were also some treasure revealers who lacked merit from past lives and therefore couldn't find what they needed, such as Rigdzin Lingpa, who was so poor that he couldn't afford the paper needed to decode the Dharma texts he revealed. Padmasambhava knew about this and hid a treasure of a donkey loaded with gold. When Rigdzin Lingpa was about to reveal it, he became quite excited, thinking, "Padmasambhava has been so kind to me—I'll get this gold treasure and be very rich!" So, as a result of his attitude, which was due to his not accumulating merit in the past, even though Padmasmbhava had provided him with a huge treasure of gold, he was only able to access a few small pieces of it. So it is very important to accumulate merit now and not delay, for later on it will already be too late.

Dharma is about the way you perceive things, and everything can be made meaningful if you transform your way of thinking. For example, when things don't go the way you want and obstacles occur at home, at your job, and so forth, if you just keep worrying about it, there will be no benefit whatsoever. It's useless to worry about such problems; instead, you should pray, "By my experiencing these difficulties, may the hardships of all beings be ripened so that their obscurations will be purified and their wishes fulfilled!" In this way, even hardships can be made meaningful and benefit others. Or when you see beautiful flowers at the market or in the hills, instead of just thinking how beautiful they are and getting attached to them, you should mentally offer them to the Three Jewels so that the experience becomes meaningful and you can accumulate merit. Likewise, while going about your daily life, you should offer whatever you see, hear, or smell—whether it belongs to you or not—to the Three Jewels and thus accumulate merit not just for yourself but for all beings. When you are working or going about your day, don't waste even the tiniest opportunity to accumulate merit by making offerings to the Three Jewels. Most people are so obscured that it never even occurs to them to offer beautiful things to the Triple Gem. They pick flowers and bring them inside to decorate their home without thinking to offer them with devotion or to dedicate that offering. You don't need to chant an offering verse; you can just mentally offer it. If you lift up these things you're offering while chanting an offering verse, people around you will probably find it very strange.

Your own body is made up of the hundred deities, so when you eat you can visualize that you make a food offering to the deities in your body mandala, such as your yidam deity and retinue. When you get new clothes, before wearing them you should offer them to the Three Jewels. After milking their cattle, Tibetan nomads will offer a few drops of the milk to the Three Jewels and then take the milk home. And farmers, when harvesting their crops, will first offer a portion of the grains. When you make tea, you can offer a drop to the Three Jewels before drinking it. You don't need to offer an entire cup of tea; just a drop or two is enough. The Three Jewels don't need any milk, tea, or clothes, but offering these things is a way to accumulate merit throughout all your daily activities and helps you to not forget the Three Jewels.

If you are not bound by dualistic thoughts, it will be easy to attain enlightenment, but if you are tightly bound by negative emotions such as attachment and aversion, it will be difficult and take a long time. To attain enlightenment, all you need to do is purify your karmic obscurations. Other than that, since buddha nature is present within us from the very beginning, there is nothing else to do. Therefore, if you pray intensely with a single-pointed mind, you can purify your karmic and emotional obscurations and attain buddhahood.

The moment we accumulate any kind of karma, unless it's purified through confession, the result will ripen within our being. Still, we have very little time to practice Dharma in a focused manner, because we typically get caught up in our immediate desire to be comfortable, and our attachment to mundane attainments easily distracts us from the Dharma.

Whatever you hear people say, pray to your guru that you don't generate wrong views and disturbing emotions and recognize that everything is merely a display of your guru. No matter how you experience the external world and its inhabitants, you should see the place as a pure buddha field and all the beings you meet as bodhisattvas, gods, and goddesses. Whatever obstacles and adverse conditions you encounter, you should see them as the path for practicing the Secret Mantra teachings.

At first it's difficult to see everything as pure, but with training you can gradually grow accustomed to it. It's very important to purify your disturbing emotions, but if you are attached to what is pleasant and beautiful and dislike what is unpleasant and ugly, you won't be able to purify your thoughts and will always be caught up in attachment and aversion. It is crucial that at all times you turn your mind toward the Dharma and try to maintain pure perception.

Our aggregates consist of the five poisons, which need to be purified through the compassionate blessings of the buddhas. When their blessings enter our being, our impure perception will gradually transform into pure perception, but without faith, devotion, and pure perception, it will be practically impossible to receive their blessings. Externally nothing obstructs us from receiving their blessings; we are obstructed by our own karmic obscurations. For instance, a clean mirror will reflect whatever is placed before it, but if it is dirty it won't reflect anything. Merely thinking that a mirror is clean won't suddenly cause it to reflect things. Likewise, merely thinking that you are pure and free of flaws and obscurations is not going to purify you. But once you are actually free of stains and obscurations and have pure perception, the blessings will naturally flow into you. Only cleaning your physical body won't help you to attain realization, and merely thinking that you are free of obscurations will not benefit you. If you examine your mind and see the quantity of disturbing emotions you have, you will see that the mind is not stable for a single moment and that if you don't reduce your disturbing emotions, they will never stop. To engage in Dharma practice, you need to be kind to yourself and know how to purify your obscurations.

Proudly thinking that you know and understand the teachings won't bring any benefit. Among all the emotions and obstructions, pride is the biggest obstacle, and there isn't a single being that isn't proud. So please take an honest, humble look at yourself, then ask the Three Jewels for their help.

OFFERINGS

IT'S VERY IMPORTANT to always supplicate your master with perfect devotion and make offerings of lamps, flowers, and so forth. Any offering you make, big or small, will be a cause for accumulating merit and purifying obscurations. But you must make offerings with pure motivation; you shouldn't offer anything with miserliness or use offerings to show what a generous person you are.

Lamp offerings purify the obscurations of ignorance, increase your life span, pacify illness, help you to perceive more in the intermediate state, and, according to Dzogchen, develop and increase your inner wisdom. In Tibet, when laypeople have problems with their business and so forth, they make large offerings of hundreds or thousands of butter lamps. They are worldly people and mainly concerned with temporary happiness and benefit, but they do receive benefit through those offerings. Since we are followers of the Mahayana path and develop bodhichitta for the sake of all sentient beings, whatever offerings we make should be for the sake of all beings to attain freedom from samsara and perfect enlightenment, which automatically includes our own benefit. The texts explain that there is tremendous benefit in offering even a single flower or single lamp for the sake of all beings.

In the past, an accomplished yogi called Jo Ben was staying in retreat and saw some of his students and sponsors approaching his retreat hut to come see him, so he arranged his shrine very nicely in order to please them. But when he sat down and became aware of his intention, he took a handful of ash and scattered it on the shrine. Another yogi who knew about this said that among all the offerings, that handful of ash was the best offering, because it was to get rid of his selfish intention. Whenever we try to tame our mind to subdue our disturbing emotions, no matter how many offerings we make to the Three Jewels or the lineage masters, the best offering is our practice.

All highly realized practitioners can immediately obtain whatever they need without any effort and just manifest things from the treasury of space. When we are practicing on the path, everything seems so difficult to accomplish, but once our realization reaches a certain level, things are naturally accomplished.

If we make offerings without stinginess and, with a pure intention, dedicate the merit to all beings, this will naturally increase our merit and not exhaust anything. Once, an accomplished yogi was traveling with his students. As it was a hot day, they stopped to rest, and the yogi asked his retinue if they wanted some curd. When they looked around, there was nowhere to get curd, but nonetheless they all said they would like some. So the master took out his skull cup and miraculously produced curd, giving them each enough so that they were satisfied.

When the Tibetan translators first went to meet Padmasambhava and offered him lots of gold dust, he just tossed it into the air as an offering to the Indian panditas. The Tibetans were quite upset that he wasted the gold they had brought all the way from Tibet to Nepal with great hardship. But Padmasambhava knew what they were thinking and said, "If you'd like some gold, please bring your bags." So they brought their bags and he filled them with sand. They wondered what they would do with the sand but didn't dare throw it away. After a while, their bags seemed to get much heavier, and when they opened them they discovered that the sand had turned into gold. Great bodhisattvas can manifest anything they wish from the treasury of space.

Near Palyul is a place called Tromthar, which was the home of a very rich family who owned about two thousand animals. This family used to make elaborate offerings to the monasteries and the different sanghas. During the Cultural Revolution, their cattle were confiscated and the family was sent to prison, where most of them perished. When the remaining family members were released from prison, some of their cattle were returned to them, but most of the herd was given to the community. They got just enough cattle for one family, but their herd increased very fast and produced a lot of milk. Usually cattle will give birth only once every two years, but their cattle gave birth once or even twice a year, so within five or six years they had nearly two hundred animals. So the communists took away most of those cattle too and gave them to other people. This family just naturally accumulated more cattle, and after this cycle repeated itself three times, the government stopped taking their cattle away. The children of that family believe that their parents had accumulated a lot of merit by making elaborate offerings to the monasteries and sanghas, and that this is why they now have such good luck and nowadays own a large herd once again.

COMPASSION AND LOVING-KINDNESS

THE GREAT INDIAN scholar Asanga spent twelve years in retreat practicing Maitreya, but after twelve years he still hadn't had a single sign or dream about Maitreya, so he gave up his retreat. On the way to town, he saw an injured dog lying on the side of the road, with maggots writhing in its festering wounds. He immediately felt intense compassion for the dog, and, wanting to save its life but not kill the maggots, he knelt down, closed his eyes, and started to remove the maggots with his tongue. When he opened his eyes, however, he didn't see the dog but Maitreya. In his shock he said, "How is it possible that after I spent twelve years devoting practice to you and going through all those hardships, you never appeared or gave me a single sign? You have no compassion!" But Maitreya answered, "It was due to your dense karmic obscurations that you couldn't see me, but I've been with you from the moment you started the practice. Now, through the intense strength of your genuine compassion for the dog and the maggots, what was left of your obscurations was instantly purified so that you can now see me!"

All beings down to the tiniest insects have buddha nature, the enlightened essence. The only difference is that their qualities have not matured. Therefore, you should respect all beings. The form one takes in subsequent rebirths depends on one's past karma and habitual patterns, which are very complicated. When you see an insect, you don't have to think, "Oh, there is a bodhisattva!" and start doing prostrations to it, but you should develop a sense of kindness toward all beings. Though you don't necessarily have to express it outwardly or verbally, you should still always mentally train in respect, devotion, and kindness.

You may be vegetarian and avoid eating meat or killing mosquitoes and other insects, but just by eating and drinking you kill many insects without being aware of it. One single leaf contains countless insects, and in the vegetables we eat there are also many tiny beings. Even the water we drink has many living beings. Buddha Shakyamuni taught that there are insects and germs everywhere, and scientists have also come to the same conclusion. Many teachings explain that even inanimate things like houses, pillars, doors, windows, ropes, brooms, and so forth contain countless invisible beings who took birth in the temporary hells. Therefore, it is taught that we should be very gentle with things; for example, we shouldn't slam a door but close it gently. So it's of great importance to continuously generate faith and devotion and develop loving-kindness to all beings, not just superficially but feeling intense care for them until tears start to flow down your cheeks. You should do this again and again, until this feeling of compassion becomes stable and arises spontaneously.

GURU YOGA

THERE ARE MANY practices related to the lamas, yidam deities, dakinis, and protectors, but the most important is guru yoga, for through it you will be able to receive your guru's blessings. From the primordial protector Samantabhadra down to your present teacher, all the buddhas and bodhisattvas attained realization by receiving the blessings of their root teacher and his lineage. There has never been a realized being who attained enlightenment without relying on a guru. So at all times, pray to your root guru and the lineage masters by supplicating them and especially by practicing guru yoga.

It is imperative to trust your master completely, without any doubt or hesitation. If sometimes you feel faith, devotion, and pure perception and pray to him, and then at other times your mind is not very stable and you lose your pure vision and devotion, you will never truly receive his blessings. If you generate faith and devotion only when things go well, then as soon as things don't go the way you want, you could even lose faith in the Dharma. So if you want to experience ultimate happiness and attain enlightenment, it is important to remember that there is no other way but to rely on a qualified master, and supreme among them is Padmasambhava. If you supplicate Padmasambhava from the depths of your heart, he will fulfill all your wishes and protect you from everything in this life and your future lives. He has the special power to protect you and grant whatever you wish to experience. As he embodies all the qualities of the past, present, and future buddhas, if you pray to him, then through his enlightened intention, you will also receive the blessings of all the buddhas.

When practicing the preliminaries, we contemplate each of the four mind changings to turn our mind toward the Dharma: the difficulty of finding the freedoms and advantages, the impermanence of life, the law of cause and effect, and the defects of samsara. We also do the extraordinary practices of refuge, bodhichitta, Vajrasattva, mandala offering, and guru yoga. But even though guru yoga is considered part of the preliminaries, it's actually the most profound practice of all, so you should dedicate yourself to it until you attain perfect buddhahood, always mingling your mind with your guru's in a state of fervent devotion. Whatever practice you do—meditating on the yidam deity, the dakini, or any other kind of practice—you should know that all yidam deities are inseparable from your guru, which is a very profound point for accomplishing the practice much faster.

You have a supreme guru who is like a wish-fulfilling gem in the palm of your hand, but if you don't supplicate with faith, devotion, and pure perception, you cannot receive the guru's blessings and awaken your potential. It's like the sun shining in the sky: if you aren't touched by the rays, you cannot feel its warmth. Likewise, if you don't supplicate your guru again and again from the depths of your heart, you cannot receive his or her blessings. If you have a lot of doubts and are not sure whether you have the right guru, one who really embodies the blessings, it will be difficult to receive any blessings, so practice carefully without deceiving yourself.

It's important to recognize that your guru's body, speech, mind, qualities, and activity are very special. Your guru's body, speech, and mind and those of the great master Padmasambhava are inseparable. Likewise, the body, speech, and mind of all the buddhas of the past, present, and future are the same as your glorious master's. This is explained again and again in the sacred texts of the Dzogchen lineage.

Whether you can actually realize the natural state of the Great Perfection depends entirely on your master's blessings entering your mind stream—there is no other means. Many practitioners with strong faith and devotion have realized their mind's natural state merely through the practice of guru yoga, so you should be confident that this practice is extremely profound and practice it continuously along with chanting the seven-line prayer. By means of your guru's compassionate blessings being transferred to you, you can attain enlightenment, but this won't happen if you have doubts or lack genuine faith in your guru and are obscured by emotional thoughts, as these will only take you further away from enlightenment. Blessings arise when you pray to your guru. This is possible because of the union of emptiness and interdependent arising, but if you don't understand this view and remain in conceptual thought without pure perception, nothing will happen. For instance, when you try to make wine, you need to add a certain type of yeast to ferment it. Mingling your mind with your guru's is like adding the yeast of the blessings of all the past, present, and future buddhas to your being.

The compassion of all the buddhas and bodhisattvas in the ten directions never wanes; it is impartial and equal for all and doesn't depend on whether one is rich or poor, beautiful or ugly, strong or weak. We have fallen into the three worlds of samsara due to our disturbing negative emotions, and we're now stuck and wander in cyclic existence, which is like a dense, dark cloud. If occasionally, like a flash of lightning through the clouds, we have some faith and devotion in the Dharma, it's due to the compassionate blessings of the buddhas and our merit accumulated during past lives.

You don't have time to do all the separate recitations of the three root deities; that's why you should concentrate on guru yoga, for it accomplishes all the deities of the Three Roots. Even if you do some yidam practice, you cannot recite more than a couple of malas, because you can't chant quickly enough and are not articulate. So the easiest way to accomplish all deities is just to supplicate your own guru and do guru yoga firm in the knowledge that the guru embodies the Three Roots.

The innumerable buddhas and bodhisattvas are always there watching us and perceiving everything we do, so you should give up all negative conduct and thoughts. Sentient beings are beyond number, but the buddhas know every detail of what every being does, good or bad. They know what you say, what you do, and what you think, so restrain your conduct and emotions, don't follow your worldly thoughts, and rest your mind in its natural flow. Consider your root guru as the embodiment of the buddhas of the three times and feel confident that your guru is always there and watches over all that you do. If you engage in negative behavior or thoughts, you should remind yourself of this, feel ashamed about it, and control your conduct.

It is said that the amount of blessings we receive is dependent upon how long and intensely we can focus our mind with one-pointed devotion. So, if you constantly supplicate again and again, the blessings will naturally flow into your being and not dissipate. Thus it is crucial to supplicate your guru from the core of your heart without getting carried away by discursive thoughts. Merely verbally expressing that you have devotion will not bring any result; you need to pray fervently and wholeheartedly. You need to purify your disturbing emotions, and there is no more effective way to do that than by devoting yourself to the practice of guru yoga.

PRACTICE

To learn Dharma, you have to study; having studied, you should then contemplate the teachings and perfect your understanding through practice. What is to be known is as vast as all the stars in the sky, so there is no way we can know everything. The Buddha taught 84,000 different teachings, and the Great Perfection alone consists of 6,400,000 teachings. It might be impossible to study them all, but if you correctly practice one of the teachings, you will be able to understand all the others and attain liberation. It's like when we have so much fruit that we can't eat it all, eating just one piece is enough to let us know what the others taste like.

Once you have settled on a practice, you shouldn't behave like a small child who sees a lovely flower and plucks it, and then upon seeing another flower and thinking that it's even better, throws away the first one and goes after the next. That will not have much benefit. Likewise, when we have received one teaching, then think that another teaching is better than that one and forget about the first one, there is not much benefit, and we end up with no result at all. We should be steady in our practice and apply what we have received instead of constantly looking for other teachings.

You may study a lot and become a great scholar, but if you can't subdue your own mind, what's the point? The best thing is to control your mind and not follow your thoughts and emotions. You might decide not to get distracted by outer appearances and to control your afflicting emotions, but this won't happen by itself. It's something you have to train in with great diligence for a long time. So always watch your mind, be careful not to follow your negative emotions, and constantly maintain your practice. Especially in places where there is a lot of trouble going on, it's much more difficult to tame your mind. If you can control your mind in such situations, you will not easily be affected by troublesome circumstances.

Many great Dzogchen yogis didn't study that much, but through their practice the qualities of the teachings naturally unfolded within them. Paltrul Rinpoche mostly stayed in retreat, but through his high realization, his enlightened qualities developed from within so that he became extremely learned. When he started to teach, he became very famous all over Kham. The Ganden Tripa, the extremely learned throne holder of the Gelukpa school, heard about Paltrul Rinpoche's fame, so he traveled to the area where Paltrul Rinpoche was staying and went to see him in order to find out if he was as smart as he was said to be. When they met, the Ganden Tripa asked Paltrul Rinpoche some questions, and the answers to all his questions were correct. Paltrul Rinpoche also asked the Ganden Tripa questions. The Ganden Tripa was extremely surprised that Paltrul Rinpoche was so learned after merely staying in a cave for years. The Ganden Tripa himself had studied for twenty to thirty years, but Paltrul Rinpoche's wisdom was much greater than his, so he asked Paltrul Rinpoche in which institute he had studied. Paltrul Rinpoche replied, "We Nyingmapas have a teaching called the Great Perfection, and when we practice that, these other teachings are not very difficult to understand." Once the realization of the Great Perfection unfolds, one will naturally understand all Dharma without studying.

Generally, the Nyingma masters and especially the past Dzogchen masters didn't study much but still became great scholars through their realization. Such a level of realization can be attained by training the channels and energies, which opens up our channels and unties the knots, but we should mainly rely on devotion, pure perception, and bodhichitta. If we fervently supplicate our master, his compassionate blessings will enter our mind and these qualities will spontaneously unfold, but we won't benefit from his blessings if we harbor doubts and wrong views and lack trust.

When doing formal practice sessions, it's very important to sit in the proper posture, because within the body there are many channels, and among these channels the heart channel and eye channel are connected. In animals, the heart channel and the heart are upside down; that's why they are so stupid, ignorant, and obscured. In human beings, the heart channel is straighter and better, and in bodhisattvas the heart channel and the heart are in the right position and placed upward, through which their realization and qualities can unfold. But this channel is not a physical organ. If it were, we could have an operation to have it put straight and put the heart upward. These are wisdom channels within our body; they cannot be seen with the eyes. But if we look upward when we do meditation practice, we can modify them into a better position, and it's taught that we should not close our eyes during practice.

In the seven postures of Vairochana, the eyes should focus four inches or a yoke's width in front, either level or below. In Dzogchen we gaze slightly upward, through which the heart channels turn upward so we perceive the wisdom on a vaster scale, and in thögal practice there are different gazes to adopt. Meditating with closed eyes is not very good, as you easily become sleepy.

Once, there were two brothers looking for a teacher, and when they found one and received teachings, both of them started practicing meditation. The older brother was very strict, and the younger one was always sitting in meditation, so his brother used to say, "Come on, let's go work. You always say you're meditating, but mostly you're just sleeping." So when you practice, it is best not to close your eyes. Thus with body, speech, and mind in the correct posture, without getting carried away by conceptual thoughts, do guru yoga again and again.

Seated in the correct posture, visualize your glorious root guru about one cubit above the crown of your head, thinking that he is really sitting there. Remind yourself that the buddhas and bodhisattvas of the ten directions and the three times, as well as all the masters, yidam deities, dakinis, and dharma protectors are inseparable from your own root teacher, and as they dissolve into you, mingling your mind with your guru's body, speech, and mind, rest in the natural state. Thus engage in guru yoga three times during the day and three times at night; if that's not possible, then at least once every morning. Supplement your practice by chanting the Vajra Guru mantra and seven-line prayer.

The four empowerments known as the vase, secret, wisdom, and precious word empowerments are of paramount importance. In general, you are not allowed to engage in the practices of Secret Mantra without first receiving the necessary empowerments. The Great Perfection, too, depends upon empowerment. Though you should receive empowerment from a qualified lineage holder, you should also receive the four empowerments at least once a day while practicing guru yoga. With engaging in the guru yoga practice and supplication, receiving the four empowerments, and then mingling your mind with your guru's, the entire path is complete and you will spontaneously receive all your guru's blessings.

So to do this, while still visualizing your root guru in the form of Guru Padmasambhava on the crown of your head, for the vase empowerment, imagine that white light emanates from his forehead and dissolves into your forehead, purifying all of your physical obscurations, the negative actions such as killing, stealing, and sexual misconduct that you have accumulated throughout all your countless lifetimes. Thus receive Padmasambhava's body blessings and, planting the seed for attaining the nirmanakaya, actualize the vajra body.

Next, for the secret empowerment, visualize red light emanating from your master's throat center, which dissolves into your own throat, purifying all of your speech obscurations and all negative verbal actions such as lying, slandering, speaking harsh words, and gossiping. Thus receive your master's speech blessings and, planting the seed for attaining the sambhogakaya, actualize the vajra speech, so that your speech becomes endowed with the sixty special qualities of sound and you attain the ability to teach, compose, debate, and so forth.

Next, for the wisdom empowerment, visualize dark-blue light emanating from your master's heart center, which dissolves into your own heart, purifying your mind obscurations, as well as all your negative mental actions such as covetousness, ill will, and wrong views. Thus receive your master's mind blessings and, planting the seed for attaining the dharmakaya, attain the vajra mind, so that your mind becomes endowed with the hundred thousand different concentrations and you attain the ability to generate love and compassion.

Lastly, visualize five-colored light emanating from your master's five places, which dissolves into your own five places—forehead, throat, heart, navel, and secret centers—purifying all your different negative actions accumulated throughout all your lives. Then your guru, who is still above your head, melts into light, which dissolves into you. Then, completely relaxing your mind, rest within the natural state. Through this you accomplish all the blessings of your master's qualities and activities, simultaneously purifying body, speech, mind, and cognitive obscurations, so that you receive the precious word empowerment and are introduced to the nature of your mind. At this point you should rest in the view of trekchö, abiding in the absolute mind nature.

Complete your formal session by dedicating the merit and making aspirations.

While eating and drinking, imagine that your guru is sitting in your throat center and offer your master whatever you eat and drink. Supplicating your master with one-pointed mind is of great importance, and no matter what you are doing, constantly visualizing and praying to your master on the crown of your head, consider that whatever karma and disturbing emotions arise, you are protected by your master's compassionate blessings. Whatever karmic obscurations, disturbing emotions, and conceptual thoughts occur, consider that your master abides at your crown center and knows your motivation and whatever you are doing, so restrain yourself.

When you lie down to sleep at night, imagine that your master descends from your crown and rests in your heart. Visualize your body to be empty inside with your master sitting on a lotus seat in your heart center emanating rays of light, which fill your entire body. Your guru's body then melts into light and dissolves into your heart center, while your mind mingles inseparably with your guru's.

While you sleep, engage in the yoga of luminosity. If you do this practice, you will have a sound and peaceful sleep without disturbing dreams, and by sleeping in this way you can transform sleep into luminosity.

I am merely giving you an indication of how to do these practices. It is important to understand the teachings properly before doing any practice, so please get the oral instructions from your teacher before attempting to do them; otherwise, you might end up like the student who had been told to visualize his guru on the crown of his head but completely misunderstood how to do it. He thought it meant visualizing himself on his master's head and carefully practiced that. One day, this student told his guru that he found it difficult to visualize himself on his teacher's bald head, as he kept slipping off. His teacher jokingly replied, "Oh, now I know why I've been having such a headache these past days—you have been doing the visualization wrong!"

Experience and realization of the true nature of mind in Dzogchen can only happen through faith, devotion, and one-pointed supplication to your guru. It is not something that is just handed from one person to another like a baton, nor can you buy it. All the past buddhas attained enlightenment through the same path, and guru yoga is the most important. Your master is endowed with many qualities, and by praying to your guru with one-pointed faith and devotion, you can realize the natural state of luminosity. Whichever deity of the Three Roots you practice, you should consider the deity to be inseparable from your own root guru. That is a special technique to swiftly receive the guru's blessings, while if you consider the deities and your master as separate, it will be difficult to accomplish anything.

It is said that if we really put effort into our practice and pray with one-pointed awareness without following conceptual thoughts, we can attain enlightenment within a week. Like the old woman in Varanasi who visualized herself as a tigress for such a long time that when she went to town everyone actually perceived her as a tigress and ran away, similarly, we can accomplish whatever we strongly focus our mind on. But we have a very hard time concentrating one-pointedly—don't we? Again and again we try, but, completely controlled by our disturbing emotions, we repeatedly get carried away by our negative thoughts and habits. So, when you notice that you have become distracted, try to subdue your mind and regain your focus. Don't indulge concepts like "This is good!" or "That is bad!" Such thinking has no benefit whatsoever—it only causes further difficulties.

Dharma practice is all about taming your mind, so you should be very careful in your conduct. Your external appearance should be proper— wear clean clothes, and so on—but most important is to have a pure mind embraced by faith and devotion. Though it is taught that you shouldn't contrive your body, speech, and mind, people don't appreciate you going around with shabby clothes and matted hair, and furthermore doing so is a disgrace to your precepts. Your external appearance should be in harmony with the mundane world, while your mind should be tamed and in harmony with others.

In your daily life, you should not give rise to anger and other negative emotions, but regard everyone with loving-kindness and be in harmony with them. While talking to others, even if you get insulted, you shouldn't get angry, and if someone gets angry with you, you should answer in a kind, loving way. I have a student in Taiwan who is from a very rich family and owns a big factory with many workers. Some of the workers listen to her and some of them don't, but either way she has to supervise the factory. When some workers do things wrong, she needs to scold them, and of course they get upset and angry if she does. So when she feels like scolding them and can't control herself, she goes to the seashore and starts complaining there, spitting out whatever she feels like saying. Once she feels satisfied, she returns to the factory, and in this way she doesn't upset anyone. That is not a bad method. It's important to reduce negative talk, so don't retaliate but try to practice patience and generate more compassion toward that person. We are followers of the Buddha, so our external conduct should be humble, peaceful, and respectful, and our mind within should be peaceful and full of respect for others as well.

Most practices are done in sessions, and we usually hear about meditation and postmeditation, but in Dzogchen there is no such thing as meditation and postmeditation: day and night we should always abide within the natural state of mind. It is taught that if we so desire, we have the potential to attain perfect buddhahood within years, months, or even days—it all depends on whether our mind is stable or not. If you don't follow your afflicting emotions for even an instant and are stable in deity visualization and abiding in the natural state, never getting carried away by negative emotions, then you can attain buddhahood within a surprisingly short time. But most of us constantly follow our afflicting emotions day and night and have no stability. Sadly, there are very few practitioners with unwavering samadhi.

We have all been wandering throughout the six realms of samsara due to our own mind, and if your mind could be slightly flexible and definitively turn toward the Dharma, your body and speech would naturally follow and you could practice easily. If your mind is not adaptable, your virtuous physical and verbal efforts won't have much effect. Just watch your mind and you'll see that it doesn't stay still for a single moment but constantly follows your negative thoughts and emotions. So try at all times to remain mindful, control your mind, and subdue your disturbing emotions.

From the moment we're born in samsara, we engage mostly in negative conduct and rarely in positive, virtuous actions. That's why it is essential to always examine our mind and not follow negative thoughts and emotions. Try to examine yourself while talking to someone and see how involved you get in following the negative emotions of attachment, aversion, and ignorance. We're usually not aware of how much negative activity is involved in just talking to someone while under the sway of our disturbing emotions. In the past, the great masters advised practitioners to stay in silence, which is the most conducive state for practicing virtue. As soon as we start a conversation, our disturbing thoughts and emotions naturally increase, and though we cannot always stay in silence, we should at least remain silent during our formal practice sessions.

If you do not apply the teachings you receive and integrate them into your mind and daily life, there won't be much benefit, so be careful and make sure to apply what you learn. There is a large monastery called Adzom Gar, and one of our monks went there for a year to receive teachings. Adzom Gar is quite cold, so people there make their tea extremely hot because it gets cold so quickly. Even though this monk had received a lot of teachings there, he didn't really apply them, so when he returned and people asked his brother if the teachings had improved him, they were told, "I don't know. Now he drinks very hot tea and is very short-tempered."

Your mind should abide in stillness and not get distracted by conceptual thoughts. Whatever you do during the day—sitting, walking, eating, sleeping, and so on—most important is to be undistracted. If you always guard your mind and abide in the natural state, you can easily attain buddhahood. So at all times try to give up dualistic thinking, and during your practice be very careful and do your best to avoid following your thought patterns. Though your physical body may sit in the proper meditation posture, if your mind keeps following thoughts, there won't be much benefit, because mind is more important than the physical body. So try to cut through your past, present, and future thoughts and abide undistractedly in the nature of mind.

In the past, there were two great Drukpa Kagyu masters, the Drukchen and Drukpa Kunlek. Drukpa Kunlek was a yogi who used to wander around most of the time, so the Drukchen said, "Let's settle down and stay in retreat for a while." So they both stayed in retreat at separate hermitages. During his retreat, the Drukchen decided that when it was over he would ride his horse to the village to beg for alms. As a mark of his rank, the horse used to wear a red feather, but the feather had gone missing, so he got to thinking that first he should go find a red feather. Drukpa Kunlek knew everything that was going on in the Drukchen's mind, so he went to see his friend, who scolded him, saying, "Why did you come here? Our retreat is not over yet!" To which Drukpa Kunlek replied, "Since you were going to town to get a feather for your horse, I thought it was!"

Out of all our thoughts, it is very difficult to have even 1 percent be of pure perception. Most of our thoughts are forms of impure vision. The moment any sort of thought occurs, it concerns either attachment, aversion, or indifference. When we meditate on the development stage in a deity sadhana, during the visualization our thoughts arise constantly, and our minds wander and get caught up in them. Even if we manage to meditate for a bit, we get carried away by thoughts again and again; that's how the mind works.

When we start practicing shamatha, Mahamudra, or Dzogchen, it's very important to be able to focus one-pointedly. If our mind keeps wandering and following thoughts, we won't accomplish anything. In worldly life too, we're always occupied with thinking about supporting ourselves and our family, constantly distracted by worries about accumulating wealth and property. But for Dharma practice, the most important thing in life is your mind, and you should turn your mind inward and constantly check it so that watching your mind becomes your main focus.

Unless your mind really mingles with the Dharma, your poisonous afflictions will keep blazing and you won't develop any good qualities. Whenever you try to meditate, many disturbances will occur, but no matter what kind of pleasant or unpleasant noises and activities may happen around you, you should try to concentrate on your practice and not get distracted. In the beginning, it will be difficult not to get disturbed by what's going on around you, but if you keep persevering in your practice, it will get easier and those things won't disturb you. This is quite an important point, for after death, when you arrive in the bardo, many sounds and noises will occur, which can be very frightening. If your mind gets disturbed then, how will you recognize them as what they are and be liberated? If you're not already used to concentrating on your practice while various sounds and activities are occurring, you will get very scared during the intermediate state, but if you're used to staying focused on your practice without getting distracted, that will be of great benefit in all situations, whether in this life or the bardo.

In general, it's considered a perfect condition when yogis and yoginis practice in isolated places. Some yogis and yoginis keep wandering from one secluded place to the other, but remaining undistracted is not a quality of the place; it's your mind that must become quiet and peaceful. If you can tame your mind, you will be at ease in all situations, so your greatest responsibility as a practitioner is to subdue your own mind. Dharma means to tame the afflicting emotions within your own mind, not to tame outer appearances. If you constantly get carried away by sights and sounds, how can you ever focus on your practice? There will always be disturbances, one noise coming from the right and another on the left.

Staying in secluded places without distraction and praying to your master in the form of Guru Padmasambhava, calling out his name, chanting the seven-line prayer and the Vajra Guru mantra with such intense devotion that tears well up, you may have a vision of Padmasambhava and receive his blessings. However, if you stay in cities or crowded places, it will be very difficult, if not impossible. Tibetan lamas often go to isolated retreat places for months and years, persevering in their practice with the simplest of comforts and food to sustain them. As their mind becomes more stable over the years, they gradually purify all their karmic obscurations and attain accomplishment in their yidam practice or whatever practice they focus on. We, on the other hand, prefer to happily stay in a comfortable place while enjoying our favorite foods, only engaging in our yidam practice for an hour or so each day.

While engaging in a yidam practice, you shouldn't get distracted even for an instant. The deity will then become very clear and your awareness unwavering. It is hard to maintain such concentration, but the calm abiding practice known as shamatha helps a lot in decreasing the disturbing emotions and keeping focus.

If you cannot stabilize your mind and remain undistracted in meditation, it makes no difference whether you are in an isolated place or not. One of our lamas found it too disturbing to be in crowded places, so to practice he preferred to stay in secluded places like caves and deserted houses. Knowing this, a yogi told him, "Whether your mind is distracted or not doesn't depend on where you stay. If your mind is relaxed and undistracted, you can stay anywhere. It doesn't depend on where your body is—that's what it means to be a yogi!" Nobody has a stable mind in the beginning, however, so it can be difficult to abide in the state of meditation, but if you truly put effort into your practice, you'll gradually get used to it and your mind will become more relaxed.

SAMAYA

DZOGCHEN INSTRUCTIONS CAN actually be quite dangerous. They are very difficult to give because they are like the fresh heart blood of the dakinis. Such teachings are not to be taken lightly, as the dakinis and Dharma protectors guard these teachings and are always watching what's going on. If you properly engage in the practice with faith and devotion and don't break your commitments, the dakinis and Dharma protectors will help and guide you on the path. But if you do not keep your commitments, they will harm you in this and future lives, and it will also cause harm to your teacher as well as your vajra brothers and sisters. Many lamas have had short lives because their students couldn't keep their commitments, and when a teacher has given many Dzogchen teachings, it will affect his or her own experience and realization.

When Khenpo Jigme Phuntsok was young, he studied with many great khenpos at Shechen and Dzogchen monasteries, and he received many instructions on Mahamudra and the Great Perfection from many very special lamas. During that time, a mother with her young daughter and a small child came to see him. The young daughter said that she was his destined consort and their union would greatly benefit his Dharma activities. She said that since he was studying in the monastery at that time, she would wait for him somewhere nearby, insisting he take her as his consort in order to benefit the doctrine. But Jigme Phuntsok told her that all he wanted to do in this lifetime was attain the rainbow body and didn't want such a connection, so he didn't accept her. Unable to convince him, she warned him that if he didn't accept her, he would have a lot of difficulties, and she left. A few days later, one of his teachers who had heard about the incident asked him why he had not respected that auspicious coincidence and accepted her. With that, Jigme Phuntsok began to think that he should have accepted the young woman's offer and began to search for her. But though he searched everywhere, she was nowhere to be found. It turned out that she was a dakini emanated in the form of a human being to benefit the doctrine. It must have been a coincidence to clear away obstacles to his life, which is often why treasure revealers stay with a dakini, but Jigme Phuntsok just wanted to continue his practice and attain the rainbow body. Later the communist invasion took place and Jigme Phuntsok experienced many difficulties. In the end, although he gave many teachings, he never had the chance to attain the rainbow body in his lifetime.

It is said that if a lama has many disciples, it increases the chances that some students will not keep their commitments, so many teachers who give Dzogchen teachings to large gatherings have difficulties and are unable to manifest the rainbow body. Even if just one or two students don't keep their sacred commitments, this can create incredible harm and obstacles to the teacher's life. For example, a very special Dzogchen master named Chadral Rinpoche never gave trekchö or thögal teachings in a gathering. He would give teachings on the four foundation practices and the three root deity recitation practices, but he never gave Dzogchen teachings in a gathering, not even to students who stayed in his three-year retreats. He may have given some trekchö or thögal teachings to a few special students, but not many and not in large groups.

The Three Excellences

Whatever practice we do, it should always be embraced by the three excellences: the excellent beginning (refuge and bodhichitta), the excellent main part (nonreferential practice), and the excellent conclusion (dedication).

The Excellent Beginning

Refuge

We begin our practice by taking refuge. The Buddha taught this simple method of devotion so that we could realize our true nature. The outer object of refuge is the Buddha, Dharma, and Sangha; the inner object of refuge is the guru, yidam, and dakini; the secret object of refuge is your body's channels, energies, and essences; and the innermost object of refuge is your mind's nature as the three kayas of essence, nature, and compassion. Until you have realized the natural state, your true nature, you must go for refuge in the outer and inner objects of refuge. If you fervently supplicate these, you will have a chance to recognize the true nature of your mind as essence, nature, and compassion.

Bodhichitta

Whatever Dharma practice you may undertake, in the beginning it's very important to generate a vast motivation based on bodhichitta. Bodhichitta is the awakened mind, our attitude, our way of thinking properly. Generating bodhichitta means that from the depths of your heart you recognize that all beings have been your parents and you need to treat them all like a mother treats her only child. As you endeavor to lead them toward enlightenment, whatever positive action you engage in should be for the benefit of all beings. Therefore, as the extent to which you are able to benefit beings depends on how vast your intention is, you should start each session with the excellent beginning: the pure motivation of bodhichitta, focusing on all your parent sentient beings with great compassion, remembering their kindness, and wishing that they be free of suffering and the cause of suffering, that they always have happiness and the cause of happiness, and that they all attain perfect buddhahood. Particularly while going through the preliminary practices known as *ngöndro*, you should really focus on this practice, because without bodhichitta there is no way to attain enlightenment. You may not yet be able to develop absolute bodhichitta within the state of emptiness, but relative bodhichitta is something you can generate, so train in it again and again.

All the teachings stress benefiting beings as numerous as space is vast, and once you have received the bodhisattva vow, you should contemplate the fact that you are now part of the noble family of bodhisattvas. You don't need to feel proud about it, but when disturbing emotions such as anger occur, remind yourself that since you belong to the bodhisattva family, it's not proper to give rise to any afflictive emotion, for you might then break your vows and wander into the lower realms.

It has been said that if we don't have bodhichitta, we have to generate it, and once we have developed it, we should not let it wane. Once it has arisen, we should nurture it and make it increase more and more. Thus you should make aspirations such as this: "May bodhichitta, precious and sublime, arise where it has not yet arisen. Where it has arisen, may it never wane but grow and flourish more and more."

Approaching Dharma with a selfish intention doesn't have much benefit. For beginningless lifetimes, we have done nothing but care about our own benefit; that's why we are still wandering in samsara. Even down to the tiniest insect, all beings just care about themselves, and there isn't a single being in this world that wants to suffer. But all these beings have been our parents in one lifetime or another, so you should generate bodhichitta for all of them without partiality, attachment, or aversion. You can't exclude certain beings because you don't like them or they cause trouble. So start out by developing bodhichitta toward your parents and gradually expand it until it encompasses all beings throughout time and space.

Great bodhisattvas such as Avalokiteshvara and Manjushri generated the wish not to attain perfect enlightenment until all beings had done so first and samsara was empty. From the beginning, Buddha Amitabha took a vow that when he attained perfect enlightenment, beings would take rebirth in his western pure land, Sukhavati, merely by hearing his name. He made aspirations that once someone was born there, they would be free of disturbing emotions and gradually attain perfect enlightenment in that very life. It is due to Amitabha's intention from the very beginning that he was able to extend his activity in such a vast way.

We can also generate such a vast enlightened mind, and by no longer cherishing ourselves, we can gradually purify our karmic obscurations. If you constantly practice bodhichitta, you will be able to become a great bodhisattva in the future. You don't need help or to depend on anyone else. For instance, in America, if you just want to build a small house, you first need to apply for a permit, and then you need to gather the resources to build the house, furnish it, and so forth. But to accomplish bodhichitta, you don't need any permits, money, or resources. All you need to do is generate it, expand it more and more, and make many prayers—it depends entirely on your own efforts.

Developing genuine devotion—and especially generating authentic loving-kindness and compassion toward all sentient beings—is the foundation of the Dharma and the basis for being able to receive your teacher's blessings. If you can develop genuine bodhichitta within your being, then whatever obscurations you have accumulated during your countless previous lives by committing the ten unvirtuous actions will be purified. The supreme antidote for purifying karmic and emotional obscurations is to stabilize bodhichitta in your mind stream. Whether you practice generosity or other virtuous acts, make offerings of millions of dollars to the Three Jewels, and so on, without bodhichitta such acts will never have much benefit. They are only really effective if done with bodhichitta—then you can accumulate a lot of merit.

In the past in Tibet, there was a lama who was very wealthy, and on the other side of the mountain was a poor lama, who was very humble but had very strong bodhichitta. In the evening, both these lamas used to do a smoke offering called *sur*, in which one makes offerings to the Three Jewels, the three root deities, all sentient beings, and the beings in the bardo. Thus pleasing the Three Jewels, satisfying the three root deities and Dharma protectors, and fulfilling the wishes of all sentient beings, one dedicates the merit, purifies karmic and emotional obscurations, and pays back karmic debts. The wealthy lama made elaborate sur offerings, offering a large variety of food and so on, which made an enormous amount of smoke. However, the spirits didn't often attend his offerings. On the other side of the mountain, the poor lama made his offering in a small container that emitted just a thin wisp of smoke, but the whole area was filled with all sorts of spirits. A person who could see spirits noticed this and was surprised that the spirits preferred the poor lama's meager offering to the lavish offering made by the wealthy lama, so he asked his guru why this was. His guru explained that it all depended on the power of their bodhichitta: The wealthy lama made very elaborate offerings, but they involved a lot of ego and pride, so because his bodhichitta was weak, the spirits didn't get much enjoyment from it. The poor lama didn't have much to offer, but due to the power of his bodhichitta, his sincerity, and the strength of his prayers, the spirits could enjoy all that they wished.

It is also important to never break the bodhisattva vow. Long ago in India, there was a king called King Prasenajit, who invited the Buddha and his followers to take their daily meal at his palace for a period of four months, during which time he offered them all his possessions. An old beggar woman who came by was filled with joy at this action and thought, "King Prasenajit has acquired all this wealth through the merit he has accumulated in the past, and now that he has met the Buddha, who is such an exceptional focus for his meritorious actions, his accumulation of merit will be truly immense. How wonderful!" Through her sincere and perfect rejoicing, she created boundless merit, and Lord Buddha was aware of this. That evening, when it was time for the dedication of merit, he said to the king, "Would you like me to dedicate to you the source of merit that you have acquired, or shall I dedicate it to someone who is more worthy of it than you?" The king replied, "Dedicate it to whomever has the greatest source of merit." So the Buddha dedicated the merit in the name of the old beggar woman. This happened three days in a row.

Exasperated, the king consulted his ministers to find a way to put an end to this, which was beginning to reflect poorly on his reign. "Tomorrow when we invite the Buddha and his followers for the offering of alms," they suggested, "we'll spill a lot of food and drink around the pots. When the beggars come to get it, we'll beat them severely to stop them from taking it." So that is what they did, and when the beggar woman came to gather up the spilled food, they beat her and she became angry, thus destroying the source of her merit. When sincerely rejoicing in the merit of the king, the beggar woman accumulated even more merit than the king himself, but as soon as she became angry, her merit declined, so that day the merit was dedicated in the name of the king. Since just arousing anger causes all our merit to decline, we should do all we can to rid ourselves of anger and the other of the five poisons.

It's very important to always apply the four disciplines of a spiritual practitioner: when someone insults you, don't insult them back; when someone hits you, don't hit them back; when someone points out your faults and slanders you, don't slander them back; and if someone is mean to you, don't be mean to them. It is important to understand and train in these. All sentient beings have been our parents in one lifetime or another, and becoming angry with them not only increases our own negative thoughts and emotions, but the other person also becomes more afflicted and deluded. So if you retaliate when someone is angry with you, both parties will only suffer, and there is no benefit whatsoever for either. It is best just to let the other person get angry while you practice patience and generate compassion. Doing so will improve your bodhichitta, and by maintaining bodhichitta you accumulate a lot of merit and will progress on the bodhisattva path. But this won't happen overnight, for since beginningless lifetimes we have been developing these bad habits. It is difficult to correct such flaws immediately, but if you work at it, you can gradually reduce them.

In worldly affairs, if you don't express yourself when you're insulted, people will say you're a coward, but from a spiritual perspective, you actually accumulate a hundred million times more merit if you keep quiet. If you give in to anger and revenge, the little merit that you possess declines. So you must choose between a bit of fame in this present lifetime or happiness in your future lives and ultimately liberation. This is like the difference between earth and sky, or between a cup of water and the ocean.

If you think about it, most of the time, day and night, we spontaneously accumulate negative actions with body, speech, and mind, and we rarely do anything truly virtuous. Even when we consume water or vegetables, we constantly harm beings, since most of the food we eat is pervaded by sentient beings. If we really reflect on the sufferings of samsara, they are utterly unbearable. We know about these frustrations but don't really reflect on them because we haven't actually seen them, so we take it easy and ignore them. Just consider one animal being captured, taken to the butcher, and killed. Even before it is dead, its skin is flayed, which makes it tremble with fear and pain, and then its flesh is cut up, which causes unbearable suffering. We don't think much about such suffering, but those who have a little compassion might say, "From now on I will never eat meat again." Every day an inconceivable number of animals are killed that way, so we need to think of it all the time and do aspirational prayers to purify their karma—that's crucial. It's good if we don't meat, but even if we do, it is still beneficial to generate compassion and do prayers for animals to be free of their karmic obscurations. This example concerns only bigger animals, but just think how many innumerable small insects there are. Even just walking around we kill innumerable invisible insects, and the number of sentient beings is inexpressible.

We only perceive larger animals, but there are innumerable microscopic organisms that we cannot see. Think about milk, for instance. We might think there is nothing wrong with drinking milk, but first of all, the milk is actually taken away from calves, and second, the milk contains countless microscopic organisms that we kill through homogenization and drinking. Water also is full of beings that are invisible to the naked eye. We think it's OK to eat vegetables, but actually every leaf is pervaded with countless insects that die when the vegetables are harvested. The same goes for meat: every part of the meat has living beings inside it. We may think that we haven't killed any animals and haven't done anything negative, but on this earth there are as many beings as there are particles of dust. Whatever we do and wherever we go, there is no place that is not filled with insects and germs. Within our own body, there are 84,000 different microbes and germs; no matter what we do, these germs and microbes suffer and die. Even when we chant wrathful deity mantras or say "Phat," many weak beings get scared and die, so it seems like whatever we do with our body, speech, and mind, we are always harming beings one way or another. But if we receive the bodhisattva vow and develop genuine bodhichitta, then even when we chant wrathful mantras it will not harm beings.

Based on our intention, everything we do can benefit beings, so it's important to continuously maintain the intention of genuine bodhichitta and not forget it. It is said that wherever space pervades, there are sentient beings, and when they die they go through the same suffering that we do, so we should pray for all of them and dedicate the merit of our practice to them so that they might purify their karma and attain liberation.

What is more, among all these beings, there isn't a single one who has not been our parent at some time or other, not merely once but many times. As Nagarjuna said, if we tried to count our mothers with balls of clay the size of juniper berries, we would run out of earth before we could count them all. We should acknowledge that while they were our parents, they showed us extreme kindness, took care of us, protected us at personal cost, and gave us food, clothing, and whatever else we needed. All these parent sentient beings are now experiencing all sorts of suffering throughout the six realms of samsara, so now that we have obtained this precious human body endowed with the eighteen favorable conditions, we shouldn't waste such a rare opportunity but use it for the sake of liberating all beings, until samsara is empty. Generating such a motivation again and again, we must integrate it into our mind, because without this precious thought of enlightenment, the path of liberation will be blocked. So you should ceaselessly endeavor to develop and integrate bodhichitta without any partiality.

THE EXCELLENT MAIN PART

The second excellence is the main practice without reference point: remaining in the nonconceptual state of emptiness.

Yidam Deity Practice

It's very important that your practice be done within the state of emptiness and compassion. While practicing your yidam deity, you should focus on the correct visualization as much as you can, clearly visualizing the details while understanding that its nature is empty and free of any truly existing quality. Nonetheless, among all Dharma practices there is nothing more profound than guru yoga, and it is crucial to understand that your yidam deity is inseparable from your root guru. When making offerings to the Dharma protectors, you should know that they are the display of your root guru. In the future, once you have realized the true meaning of the Great Perfection, at that time your master's body, speech, and mind—your guru's essence, nature, and compassion—and your own body, speech, and mind will really mingle. If you haven't been introduced to your true nature, then you should simply be confident that they are inseparable. However, whatever Dharma practice you do, the main aim is to recognize your mind's intrinsic nature.

If you perceive the deities as being separate from your guru, they will appear separate and won't lead to accomplishment. Instead, you should recognize that all deities are one in nature, inseparable from your master; if you do, then it will be easy to receive the blessings and accomplishments. All the mahasiddhas of the past approached their practice in this way, but unfortunately many people think that the deities are all individual entities and practice them separate from their guru. Women might think it's quicker to attain accomplishment by practicing a female deity such as Tara or Vajrayogini, and men might think it's quicker to attain accomplishment by practicing a wrathful male deity, but all deities are one in their absolute nature. According to a saying, "Tibetans try to practice a hundred different deities and can't accomplish even one, but Indians practice just one deity and accomplish it." Many siddhas in India spent their entire lives practicing just one deity and accomplished it. Due to the kindness of Guru Padmasambhava, there are many different sadhanas of many different deities in Tibet, but most people don't accomplish any because they do too many different practices.

In general, pride is something we should get rid of; it is an obstacle that blocks the development of positive qualities, but in practicing the development stage and visualizing yourself as the deity, one of the main points is to maintain the pride of being the deity. Being convinced that you are really the deity is actually an antidote to pride. The visualization of the deity should develop within the state of emptiness and compassion. When you visualize a wrathful deity, either with one face and two arms or with three heads, six arms, and so forth, unless it is embraced by emptiness, it will be just an ordinary appearance. If you don't practice the visualization of a wrathful deity within the state of emptiness and compassion, then even if you think that you are such-and-such wrathful deity with wide-open eyes and loudly chant the mantra, there will be no benefit; it could even lead to birth as a ghost or spirit. Though you think you are a particular deity, you should not get carried away by conceptual thought but remain in the state of emptiness and bodhichitta united.

If tantrikas who meditate on wrathful deities and loudly chant the mantra use the practice to harm and kill others, it is no different from ordinary beings killing and harming others. In fact, it causes even more severe negative karma. All wrathful deities emanate not through anger and wrath but out of their compassion. For instance, the wrathful emanation of the deity of compassion, Avalokiteshvara, appears not out of anger but through compassion to tame all those who are difficult to tame.

If we practice a wrathful deity, with genuine loving-kindness and compassion manifesting the yidam deity from the state of emptiness, there will be power and benefit, but if we practice a wrathful deity in an ordinary, afflicted state of mind, we may develop problems later on.

In general, worldly talk just causes our afflicting emotions to increase. Negative emotions will always stir our mind, and when we get involved in conversation, they just increase, so it's better not to engage much in conversation. While talking, we naturally give in to attachment and aversion and increase our negative emotions. Therefore, while chanting the sadhana and reciting the mantra, it is best to remain silent; that way the blessings of the Dharma can enter our speech. If you keep talking while doing the recitation, you will not accomplish the practice and many obstacles will be invoked. To receive the Buddha's speech blessings and accomplish the power of enlightened speech, you should remain silent while doing recitation. Once you receive the Buddha's speech blessings, whatever you say will benefit others and is very good.

All beings, even the tiniest insects, possess buddha nature, so when doing a yidam deity practice, you should always consider any sound that you hear—wind, water, rainfall, people, and so forth—to be the mantra; your surroundings to be your yidam deity's pure land, such as the Copper-Colored Mountain in the case of Padmasambhava; and all beings to be the yidam deity. By doing that, you will receive your yidam deity's blessings. Based on the primordially pure nature of phenomena as it is, approaching the world in that way will develop your pure perception.

Chö: Cutting Through

When we do the practice called *chö*, we let go of our ego-clinging and offer our body to the Three Jewels, gods, demons, and evil forces in order to repay our karmic debts. *Chö* means "cutting through," and what we cut through is our clinging to the self. But nowadays there is a tendency for chö practitioners to try to get rid of ghosts, saying that they must chase away a ghost from a certain place. With this approach, however, instead of getting rid of their ego-clinging, they just accumulate more thoughts.

In the evening it is good to do chö practice. If you do the practice properly without distraction, then you can sever your ego-clinging, but if many thoughts occur, then it won't be effective. You might enjoy doing chö practice, but if you can't get rid of conceptual thoughts, it's of no use. You may have a damaru and bell and chant well, but if your practice is not very good, it can be dangerous. For example, some people like to challenge haughty spirits who can cause a lot of trouble, and then they'll say that there are all sorts of spirits who do all kinds of malicious things, but this only proves that they didn't cut through their ego. Their chö crumbled and their conceptual thinking got stronger, so in such cases the practice actually does more harm than good. In real chö practice, conceptual thought must be cut through, and whatever gods or spirits appear are just visual appearances, whose nature is emptiness.

To practice chö, you start, of course, with refuge and bodhichitta, then as you utter *phat*, your consciousness shoots out of the crown of your head and transforms into Vajravarahi the size of a pea, with one face and two arms, colored red, holding a curved knife in her right hand and a skull cup in her left, and adorned with bone ornaments. As you utter *phat* again, she becomes the size of a finger, and as you say *phat* again she becomes the size of one cubit, and then with *phat* once more she becomes huge, filling all of space. The purpose of increasing the size from small to large is to train in clear visualization. With a single blow of her curved knife, she slices off the skull of your corpse, and, placed in the space in front, it becomes as vast as the three world systems. With another single swing of her curved knife, she peels off your skin, lifts up your corpse, and throws it all into the skull cup, and with another motion she transforms the impure contents into the five meats and the five nectars. Under the skull cup are three human heads—wet, dry, and semidry, symbolizing the three kayas—and as the fire blazes beneath the skull cup, the contents turn into wisdom nectar.

Then as you say *phat phat*, innumerable identical forms of Vajravarahi emanate from your heart, holding a spoon in their right hand and a skull cup in their left. Visualizing countless lineage masters, yidam deities, dakinis, and protectors in the sky before you, with *phat* imagine that the Vajravarahi emanations scoop out the blessed contents and make offerings to the yidam deities and lineage masters. Again as you say *phat*, they make offerings to the dakinis and protectors, and feeling that they are very pleased, you receive their blessings and accomplishments.

Then saying *phat*, make offerings to all the local deities and worldly protectors; with another *phat* offer to the nonhuman beings; with another *phat* make an offering to all the beings of the six reams; and with another *phat* make an offering to all the harmful, negative forces to whom you owe karmic debts. Imagine that the objects of offering—the lineage masters, yidam deities, dakinis, and protectors—are pleased and fulfilled, that the nonhuman beings are satisfied, that the wishes of the beings of the six realms are fulfilled, that you have repaid all your karmic debts and loans accumulated since beginningless time, and that all harmful spirits are content and won't do any more harm.

Then as you utter *phat phat phat*, all the invited guests return to their own abodes and you rest in the nature of emptiness beyond the three concepts of someone offering, anyone being offered to, and the act of offering. Conclude by dedicating the merit to all beings with the dedication prayers and, most important, generate compassion and loving-kindness to all beings.

I have provided only a brief description here to give you an idea of how chö practice is done. Before actually doing the practice, you must receive the empowerment and oral instructions from an authentic lineage holder. Padmasambhava predicted that when demon activity flourishes, people will do chö practice wrong. In the practice of chö, we chant *phat* many times, which is supposed to cut through conceptual thought. There is a saying in Tibet that if you don't know the meaning of *phat*, you'll lose your own life.

THE EXCELLENT CONCLUSION: DEDICATION

Whatever Dharma practice or virtuous actions we have engaged in, it's important to conclude with the excellent conclusion: dedicating merit and making aspirations. Otherwise, whenever we get carried away with our disturbing emotions, any virtue we have accumulated will be completely consumed in the flames of the five poisons. Once we have dedicated a virtuous act, it is sealed and the merit can't be destroyed by any negative emotions. The Dharma practices we engage in always include a dedication at the end, so naturally we do them, but you should also dedicate any other virtuous actions you perform, since you don't know when they might be exhausted due to your afflicted mind. It doesn't matter whether the act is big or small— it must be dedicated for the sake of all beings. Even if you offer just a single incense stick or one flower or recite a single mantra, it must be sealed by dedicating it to the benefit of all beings.

Whatever practice you do, guru yoga or yidam deity practice, your intention might be to accomplish the practice as quickly as possible, but there will be no result from doing so. Only when you have genuine loving-kindness, immeasurable compassion, unwavering devotion, and pure perception can you purify your karmic obscurations and get some signs. If you just practice in the hope of getting signs and experiences, it's not going to happen. When your body, speech, and mind fully trust the Three Jewels without any doubt and you practice with single-pointed devotion and pure perception, you can get some results.

So you should always dedicate all virtuous actions that you engage in, and your dedication should be for all sentient beings to attain ultimate happiness. Dedicating your virtue to only your own parents and family in this life doesn't have much strength. Of course it is good to dedicate the merit to your parents and family, but all beings have been your parents in one lifetime or another, so you should dedicate any merit you have accrued to liberate them all from the suffering of samsara.

PART THREE

PERSEVERANCE

YOU MIGHT FIND it difficult to engage in some of the practices that you have been taught, but if you do them with faith and devotion, any hardships you undergo will purify your obscurations, so you shouldn't lose heart. For example, the yogic exercises known as *tsalung* can be quite demanding, but over time as you practice them, they will gradually get easier and you'll slowly get better at them. Anything in this world can be accomplished through training. All the past masters spent their entire life doing practice—that is how they attained realization. Think about the incredible hardships that Milarepa had to go through, just so he could realize the true nature of his mind. Likewise the omniscient Longchen Rabjam went through many hardships as well. For example, while receiving teachings from his master Kukuraja, all he had to wear was a wool sack, which served as both his clothing and his bedding. He also had very little food to eat, but nevertheless by continuing his practice he attained accomplishment. All the great vidyadharas and masters from the past went through similar hardships to practice the Dharma in order to attain accomplishment, so if you experience hardship during your practice and get discouraged, thinking you can't do it, just remember that the ultimate result is the attainment of buddhahood, and generate diligence. Otherwise, the only thing to do is continue wandering in samsara, which is nothing but endless suffering.

Dharma practice cannot be accomplished in a few months. Such a thing is extremely rare. If you want to accomplish practices like tsalung quickly and push yourself too much, your body won't be able to handle it and you will become physically or mentally ill. If you don't get an immediate result, thinking that Dharma practice has no effect or benefit and wanting to give it up will corrupt your commitments. The most important points are to stay relaxed, remain diligent in your practice, and observe your own mind. It's important to receive Dharma teachings, but it's more important to look inward to check how many negative or virtuous thoughts arise in your mind, examine what you're doing to see whether you have violated your precepts, and correct yourself accordingly. Worldly people usually complain about the faults of others, judging them as right or wrong, but that's not the way to practice Dharma. Instead, you should watch your own mind and examine it at all times. If your mind is positive and pure, it's easy to practice Dharma. We are always told to have faith and devotion, not harbor wrong views or doubts, and remain steadfast. If any of the five poisons arise, you should subdue them so that they lose their strength. Once they lose their strength, they dissolve into emptiness—there's nowhere else for them to go.

We shouldn't be impatient about getting results from our practice. One time in India, a foreigner came to see Chadral Rinpoche with a beautiful statue of Padmasambhava and asked him to bless it. Then he went to do his preliminaries and did many prostrations to the statue. But he became so fanatical about his practice that he not only didn't get any good signs or dreams, he also seriously damaged his knees. Expecting results from the practice in a short time, he became very impatient and ended up directing his anger at the statue. So he took it back to Chadral Rinpoche, saying that he didn't want it anymore, and gave up his Dharma practice. Hoping to get realization within a short time typically ends badly.

We do a little practice from time to time and get some experiences and then think we are almost enlightened, but the truth is that it's very hard to attain even the first bodhisattva level—and then we have to get from the first level up to the tenth! Among the great masters from the past who attained realization in a short period was the great scholar Mipham Rinpoche. He practiced wrathful Manjushri for thirteen years without ever coming out of his cave; he never washed and never even took off his belt until he attained supreme accomplishment. That is the way we too should practice.

It is said that by practicing the outer tantras like kriya, upa, and yoga tantra, we need three, seven, or sixteen lifetimes to attain enlightenment. It is said that for the inner tantras, like the Great Perfection, we can attain enlightenment within one lifetime, and supreme individuals can do so in three years, six years, or twelve years. The Great Perfection is the fastest path. But please remember that the negative actions you have accumulated are not just from a few lifetimes but from countless aeons, so it is going to take some time to purify them.

You don't practice for just a few days, a few months, or a few years. It's like eating: you need some food every day. Practicing hard for a few days and then giving in to laziness and stopping your practice is a big mistake. In Tibetan we have the expression *atsar*, which we use when we come across someone who feels very familiar to us the moment we meet them, as if we have known that person for a long time. But once we get used to the person, we don't stay in touch and create a distance between ourselves so that the relationship is lost. Likewise, in the beginning, when the teachings are fresh and new, you might feel very excited and want to practice all the time, but then gradually you get lazy and give up your daily practice. Without continuity, however, you won't make much progress or get much in the way of results. But if you practice every day throughout your entire life, then even if you don't attain realization in this life, at least you can attain a degree of freedom so that you have a choice to be reborn here or not.

If we calculate the life span of a human being, most people live about eighty years, but out of that we spend about forty years sleeping and the other forty years primarily involved in worldly activities and caught up in the five poisons. So out of our eighty years, at the very most we'll spend five years of our life practicing Dharma. Even though the only thing that really benefits us is the Dharma, while we do a little bit of practice, our mind is still totally caught up in negative thoughts and emotions. I don't really need to tell you this—just check your own mind and you'll find out. No matter how much effort you put into worldly activities, the outcome will never be stable or permanent, but if you really practice the Dharma continuously and accomplish it, the fruition will be permanent and will not deceive you. Though it seems very difficult to get rid of your disturbing emotions, once you become aware of them, it really isn't that hard to subdue them. No matter how strong your negative emotions are, if you really work at it, there's nothing you can't accomplish. If you examine the quality that a negative emotion has, it may give you some temporary pleasure, but ultimately, by giving in to your disturbing emotions you'll end up wandering in samsara endlessly.

You should never feel that you have done enough practice and be content. If you have a little bit of knowledge or experience in the practice, you might think that you are quite special, but if you develop this kind of pride, you will just become worse, not better. The Dharma is something you must practice continuously without limit or satisfaction, and you must keep increasing your diligence. There is never a time when you can say, "Now I'm liberated!" But if you stick to it, through the power of the Dharma sometimes you will honestly feel that you are independent and have a bit of freedom, which means your practice is going well.

Every single one of the great masters who attained supreme realization thoroughly contemplated the four mind changings—the freedoms and advantages of human birth, death and impermanence, karma and result, and the sufferings of samsara—and they all continued to practice one-pointedly throughout their entire life. If you start to practice and go to a secluded place in the mountains or forest to practice, after a while you will realize that all your fears and frightening thoughts are disappearing, and you might attain some signs like mundane foreknowledge, but this is not stable and can disappear. If you practice with great diligence, you'll gradually develop unconditioned foreknowledge, through which you can clearly know when your karmic obscurations will be purified and when you will attain liberation, so you need to go through all these experiences before attaining enlightenment.

Through practice, your enlightened nature will gradually manifest. Now, you might think that since the enlightened nature and its qualities are within us, we can just have some kind of operation to have it revealed, but mind is something invisible; nobody can perform surgery on the mind. When we talk about obscurations and afflictions, it's not some kind of black ball containing negative things: karma is naturally bound to us, but it's invisible.

The more Dharma practice we do, the more we can purify our obscurations and reveal our own enlightened nature. It all depends on us, ourselves. You might complain that you have practiced a certain deity but couldn't accomplish it, or that you did many supplication prayers but nothing happened. This is due to having doubts about whether you will accomplish it. We constantly get carried away by our doubts and uncertainties.

When the great siddhas of the past received transmissions and instructions from their masters, they spent their entire life practicing with great trust, faith, and devotion, and through their intense perseverance, they attained liberation within one lifetime. At the beginning, they were the same as we are, their minds filled with poisonous afflictions, but through great courage, diligence, and perseverance, they attained realization and became an object of refuge themselves. So you shouldn't lose hope.

We spend our entire lives engaged in mundane affairs and never stop working. Our attachment to comfort and wealth causes us many problems, but still we never stop. All our work is just to obtain a little comfort in this life—other than that, there is no benefit. Even if we have a job and earn some money, we tend to fritter it all away. Though our jobs are tough and we keep complaining, we just keep working without considering how meaningless it all is and letting it go. Then, when we engage in Dharma practice and sit through long teachings and rituals, we get tired and complain how uncomfortable we are. On the other hand, all the great vidyadharas of the past had hardly any food, yet they practiced in caves for months and years with little more than the most basic necessities. They didn't care about comfort and never gave up, undertaking hardships for the sake of the Dharma at the cost of their own life. These days there are very few practitioners who are willing to practice like that. If we experience even the slightest difficulty for the sake of the Dharma, we are ready to quit.

If you have any Dharma qualities, this will benefit you and all sentient beings on a vast scale, both temporarily and ultimately, so you should always practice the Dharma correctly. That is our main responsibility in this life. Now that we have obtained this precious human birth endowed with the freedoms and advantages, which is extremely difficult to obtain, as taught through causes, examples, and numbers,* it's essential to generate effort and practice the core of the Dharma. As much time and effort as you put into your Dharma practice, day and night, you will accumulate that much merit and develop your qualities and capacities. Anyone can study, practice, and accomplish the Dharma; it makes no difference whether you are good or

---

* Reflecting on images that show how difficult it is to find the freedoms and advantages, the Buddha said that to obtain a human existence with the freedoms and advantages is more difficult than it would be for a blind turtle, coming up from the depths of the ocean once every hundred years, to put its head by chance through the opening of a wooden yoke tossed around by huge waves on the surface. The difficulty of obtaining human birth is also compared to getting dried peas thrown at a smooth wall to stick to it, or to balancing a pile of peas on the tip of an upright needle, which is hard enough with even one single pea!

Reflecting on numerical comparisons, it is said that if the inhabitants of the hells were as numerous as stars in the night sky, the pretas would be no more numerous than the stars visible in the daytime; that if there were as many pretas as stars at night, there would only be as many animals as stars in the daytime; and that if there were as many animals as stars at night, there would only be as many gods and humans as stars in the daytime. It is also said that there are as many beings in hell as specks of dust in the whole world, as many pretas as particles of sand in the Ganges, as many animals as grains in a beer-barrel, and as many asuras as snowflakes in a blizzard, but that gods and humans are as few as the particles of dust on a fingernail.

Reflecting on the causes, these freedoms and advantages do not come by chance or coincidence, they are the result of an accumulation of merit and wisdom built up over many kalpas. The great scholar Trakpa Gyaltsen says, "This free and favored human existence, is not the result of your resourcefulness, it comes from the merit you have accumulated."

bad, rich or poor. Everything depends on the amount of perseverance you put into the practice.

For the sake of accomplishing mundane studies and activities, we face so many hardships and put forth so much effort for so many years that if we were to put the same amount of effort into our Dharma practice, we would attain the rainbow body. But because we lack merit, we cannot arouse enough interest and feel inspired enough to persevere in the practice. Even reciting one mala of mantras makes us weary, because we lack merit and don't have enough training from our past lives.

My own root guru was extremely special. He had great blessings and immense compassion. During his entire life, he never got involved in ordinary conduct or mundane conversation, and whether traveling or staying home, he never failed to practice during the four periods of the day. When he had to give some advice about the monastic rules, discipline, or whatever, he would only say it once and never repeat it. He never ate dinner; in the morning his attendant would bring breakfast and at noon lunch, and if he had anything to tell his general secretary, he would discuss only that and never speak of anything else. He was imperturbable and would always sit in meditation posture like a statue, immovable, never turning right or left.

Conduct

WE MIGHT BE able to hide our negative conduct from others and deceive them, but the enlightened buddhas and the law of cause and effect cannot be deceived. Though the buddhas and bodhisattvas will not punish us, through the law of cause and effect we'll experience the results of our negative actions by falling into the lower realms and continuing to wander in samsara, so it's very important to be careful in our conduct.

You must constantly control your behavior and maintain discipline. In Tibet, I studied with a great Dzogchen yogi named Khenpo Nuden, from whom I received the transmission of a commentary on the root tantra of Anuyoga, the *Scripture of the Great Assemblage*, consisting of four volumes. There were five of us receiving it, and we were respectful, behaved very well, maintained discipline, and took care not to disturb him. There was one khenpo who coughed much of the time, which made quite a bit of noise. In the morning, before starting the class, someone used to ring the gong, but one morning there was no bell. We went and asked why nobody rang the gong and were told that the master was angry and had told them not to ring it. So I went to see Khenpo Nuden and said, "It's time to ring the gong."

But he just said, "No."

Then I asked him if he was sick, but he again said, "No."

And when I asked if he had had a disturbing dream, he repeated, "No."

After I asked him several such questions, he explained why he didn't want to teach: "You students don't behave respectfully."

"But we are all trying to be very respectful and maintain good discipline," I replied. "So what's wrong?"

"That one khenpo is always coughing and clearing his throat as if he's showing off or something!"

I explained that we had already asked him to try not to cough so loudly during the teaching, but it was an illness and he couldn't help it. Finally Khenpo Nuden acquiesced, so we renewed our commitment to maintain strict discipline, and he gave the bare minimum of teaching.

You should be very careful when going to see a master, no matter who it is. Generally, in the presence of a master, you shouldn't cough loudly, talk to one another, make noise, get up and sit back down, and so on. You also shouldn't go into the master's presence when you have a lot of disturbing emotions and thoughts. There is an entire text devoted to explaining the detailed conduct for relying on one's master.

Whatever you do, it's always best to first consult your guru so that you don't have to decide it on your own. If you are even slightly at odds with your guru, this will hinder your progress on the path. Once you have realized the stages of the path, you can do whatever you want, but to attain perfect enlightenment, you need to rely on a master, so you must be respectful. Practicing the Dharma teachings through which perfect enlightenment can be attained is something that cannot be bought even if you have millions of dollars, and if there is even a slight breach of samaya, you won't be able to attain realization, because the life force of the practice is the samaya.

We consider ourselves to be Dharma practitioners, so it's important to conduct all our actions of body, speech, and mind in a peaceful, subdued manner. However, if we appear peaceful while our mind is filled with disturbing emotions, we are not really tamed. Of the three gates—body, speech, and mind—it is the mind that is most important. All of our thoughts are influenced by our disturbing emotions and naturally keep changing every instant. Our main responsibility is to continuously subdue our disturbing emotions, constantly examine our mind, and keep correcting our attitude, not only on a gross level but right down to the most subtle.

If each of us could practice, attain realization, and be free of the sufferings of samsara, we would fulfill the wishes of all the buddhas of the three times. All the buddhas, day and night, always know each and every positive and negative thought and action of every individual being without forgetting a single detail, which is due to their omniscient mind. If, on the one hand, we constantly give rise to negative thoughts and actions in the presence of the buddhas and, on the other hand, supplicate them, it would seem a bit strange, but if our conduct is such that we don't need to feel ashamed about it, the buddhas will be pleased, right? For us there is a difference between obvious and hidden, but for the buddhas there is no such distinction. Their omniscient mind knows everything at every moment. The buddhas and bodhisattvas never get angry. Their only concern is for every being to exhaust their disturbing emotions and attain buddhahood. We might think that we can deceive the buddhas and bodhisattvas, but they know everything we do, so we cannot possibly fool them.

ACCOMPLISHMENT

IF YOU DO guru yoga again and again, you'll get more familiar with it so that it will become much easier. It's even possible that experiences such as bliss, clarity, and nonthought will arise, but a good practitioner shouldn't expect signs or experiences to come. If you continue to do good practice, it doesn't really matter whether you get signs or not, but if any do arise, you should just let them be and not get caught up in them. If you boast about your experience, it will only harm your practice, so it's better not to talk about such things except with your teacher. The real sign and result is when your disturbing emotions subside and your mind becomes more relaxed and peaceful.

In the West, some people have asked me if I think they are realized, but if you are about to get enlightened, you don't need to ask anyone. You will know that yourself! Bodhisattvas who are about to become enlightened can transform material things into immaterial things and the other way around; they can walk through rocks or fly in the sky, and they know the degree of their realization. Non-Buddhists like Hindus can develop similar qualities and show conditioned miracles, so really these are not so amazing.

In the past, Karma Chakme Rinpoche spent about six years going around giving teachings, and one time at a place called Tserung in Gojo he met an old man who told him that he must be a great master and should show some miracles as a sign of accomplishment. The old man justified this by explaining that Karma Pakshi had once been there and showed some miraculous signs, due to which many people gathered and became very devoted to him. In reply, Karma Chakme Rinpoche gave the old man a text that he had composed and said, "I can't show any miracles, and clairvoyance is nothing to be amazed at. Even some worldly spirits can squeeze rocks and bend iron with their hands, and certain birds like ravens have strong clairvoyance. My greatest miracle is that I've maintained the pratimoksha vows without even the slightest breach, and the perfect bodhichitta that I constantly practice is the greatest miracle I can perform." Likewise, you should keep your vows in a pure way, maintain pure conduct, not create wrong views through conceptual thoughts, and develop stability in your mind.

Karma Chakme Rinpoche was a great bodhisattva who used to teach people just one page of text, though his collected works of commentaries consisted of about one hundred volumes. Many of these writings were lost during the Cultural Revolution in Tibet, but still about sixty volumes remain. Though this great master really benefited beings through his teachings, people would still prefer to see a few miracles. Even today, when people see miracles or examples of clairvoyance, they think it's really special. But the greatest miracle is to mingle your mind with the Dharma, generate bodhichitta, and maintain the precepts in a pure way. That is a true miracle!

Visions and Obstacles

Though right now you haven't completely realized the view of trekchö and don't know how to let be in meditation, just try to concentrate without getting carried away by your thoughts, and this will help to settle your mind. You have to tame the mind, which is like a wild elephant running around. The more stable your mind gets, the easier it is to practice, and it will become even easier when you start meditating according to the Great Perfection. Once you start practicing meditation, you may have experiences like bliss, clarity, and nonthought; predictions; or visions of your yidam deity; but you should just let such experiences be and not become attached to them. Many Dharma practitioners, however, get caught up in such experiences, which only creates obstacles. What we really need to do is go beyond dualistic thoughts, progress on the path, and traverse all the levels of a bodhisattva.

There are four principal maras: the mara of the aggregates, the mara of emotional disturbances, the mara of the Lord of Death, and the mara of the divine child. Of these four, the most difficult to tame is the mara of the divine child, which is no other than the demon of arrogance. Due to this demon, we have all sorts of splendid experiences and indulge in them, which causes a lot of problems. You could have a vision that you'll be born in a certain place where there are treasures that you will reveal and then get all excited, thinking that you are special. There are many stories of practitioners doing retreat in secluded places and having visions and prophecies of dakinis saying that they should stay together with a certain consort in order to spread their Dharma activities, reveal treasures, and so on; these are called "the dakinis' challenging experiences." Unless you have high realization, it's very difficult to determine the authenticity of such predictions. If they are not authentic, you are being deceived by the demon of arrogance, and if you think they are authentic, the only place you will go is the lower realms.

Once, a student of the great Nyoshul Lungtok Rinpoche was staying in retreat about two days' walk from the great lama's residence. While there, he received a dakini's prophecy telling him to connect with a certain consort in order to reveal a treasure that would benefit many beings. At first he thought it was just an obstacle and didn't pay attention to it, but it kept reoccurring, so finally he decided to go ask Nyoshul Lungtok about it. When he arrived, he found Nyoshul Lungtok outside doing circumambulations. Before he had a chance to say anything, his guru looked at him and said, "Obstacles, obstacles, obstacles!" Understanding that the prediction was nothing but an obstacle, the yogi didn't bother saying anything more about it. He just returned to his hermitage and continued his practice.

All kinds of thoughts can occur while we're practicing the Dharma. When pleasant thoughts occur, we tend to follow and enjoy them, but no matter what good or bad thoughts occur, don't chase after them, or your practice will never be successful.

When I was quite young and was staying with my teacher, I used to have a lot of visions of deities, like the mandala of the Eight Sadhana deities, Vajrakilaya, and so forth. When I asked my teacher about it, he told me just to generate devotion, receive empowerment, and not be attached to my visions. I did as he said, and eventually the visions subsided.

When Tibet was taken over by the communists and I was about to leave the country, I heard many voices saying things like, "You must leave now!" and "You should do this, it's time to go!" but I didn't pay much attention to them. The Dharma protectors tried to warn me too, telling me that I should leave as soon as possible, but I didn't pay them any heed either. If I had, I wouldn't have experienced so much trouble trying to escape. Anyway, whatever good or bad thoughts occur, I usually don't follow them, which seems the safer choice to make.

One time, a monk brought a small piece of red cloth to my teacher Palyul Choktrul Rinpoche, who was very young at the time, and asked him to make it into a protection cord. Rinpoche took the cloth, threw it in the fire, then took the ashes and ate them. He then pulled a knotted thread from his mouth and gave it to the monk. So the monk took the protection cord and was so happy and excited that he went around telling the other lamas what happened. When Choktrul Rinpoche's root guru, Lhatrul Rinpoche, heard about this, he scolded Choktrul Rinpoche and told him never to show off his power, as it would create a lot of obstacles for his Dharma activities.

If we want to go to New York but along the way find a really nice place and just stay there, we'll never reach New York. It's the same with attaining enlightenment: we are on the path to buddhahood, but if we indulge in pleasant experiences along the way and get stuck there, we won't progress on the path and will never reach enlightenment.

You're not practicing Dharma to have visions of deities or experience bliss. You want to accomplish ultimate buddhahood, don't you? If so, you should be able to accomplish it without any obstacles, because now that the Dzogchen teachings are flourishing, you have the opportunity to attain enlightenment in this very lifetime, and if not, then you should at least attain liberation within three lifetimes. Once you have received the mind teachings and correctly train in them, you can purify your karmic obscurations and attain the ultimate result relatively quickly and easily. You don't need to buy it, borrow it, or go anywhere to find it; it is present within your own mind and not difficult to attain. If you want to buy gold, you need to put forth a lot of effort to get it, but to reveal the qualities within yourself is just a matter of purifying your obscurations. There will always be a few good and bad signs along the way, but you don't practice in order to get signs or have visions. You practice in the hope of attaining buddhahood, so develop faith and devotion and diligently practice until you have attained nothing less than the ultimate goal!

MENDRUP

THE TRADITION OF making the sacred medicine known as *mendrup* has been passed down in an unbroken lineage since the time of Shantarakshita, Padmasambhava, and King Trisong Deutsen. The name in Tibetan is *dudtsi chömen*: *dud* means the disturbing emotions, and *tsi* is the transcendental wisdom that purifies the disturbing emotions.

If you catch a cold or flu and take some of this sacred medicine, it will help to get rid of it. Mendrup contains thousands of different medicinal substances and has no poisonous substances whatsoever. It also contains many other substances that were revealed by treasure revealers over the centuries. It has thousands of relic substances from different buddhas, mainly from Buddha Shakyamuni and Kashyapa. It also contains flesh from a Brahmin saint born seven times, which can cause instantaneous experience and realization. It contains great blessings and is very expensive to prepare. Because it contains gold, silver, and many other precious stones, to make one batch in India costs between 300,000 and 600,000 rupees.* Once the recipe has been prepared, we then have to bless it by practicing a special sadhana for at least ten days and nights. If the preparation and practice have been successful, various signs occur. For example, while it is still wet in the containers, the scent can be smelled a few kilometers away. Other signs are things such as rainbows appearing in the sky, fire burning in the mandala, or the quantity naturally doubling or tripling. The effect of this sacred medicine is always beneficial, and it has no negative side effects whatsoever. Whatever poisonous effect there could be from the ingredients is extracted at the beginning.

One of the unique ingredients is the flesh of a seven-times-born Brahmin saint. The reason for this is that there was once a king in India who needed

---

* Approximately US$4,500 to $9,000.

to eat fresh meat every day, as without fresh meat his meal would not satisfy him. One day, his daughter went out to buy some, but because of the heavy rains she couldn't find any in the market. If she didn't get any meat, her father would scold her badly, so on her way home she found the body of a dead child near the road and cut off some of its flesh, cleaned it, and had it prepared for her father's meal. It happened that the dead child was a seven-times-born Brahmin saint, and after the king ate some of the flesh, he had amazing experiences of clairvoyance and realization, so he asked his wife where the meat came from. The queen told him that their daughter had gotten it in the market, but when he summoned his daughter, she didn't dare to tell him what he had actually eaten. So he put a knife to her chest and told her to speak frankly or he would kill her. Having no choice, she told her father where the meat had come from, and he immediately had her bring the body of the dead child to the palace. The king cut the rest of the child's flesh into small pieces, mixed it with different types of medicines, and hid it as a treasure. By eating such special flesh from a seven-times-born Brahmin saint, one will not fall into the lower realms. But this only works with this special meat, not from eating any child's flesh; in fact, eating human flesh creates even more negative karma than eating animal meat.

If someone is seriously ill, taking some mendrup can help a lot, and it's really beneficial to give some to people who are about to die, as then they won't go to any of the three lower realms. Giving buddha relics to someone who is about to die also has great benefit. In places where you can hear spirits and ghosts, they will be pacified if you burn some mendrup.

Mendrup is also added to the water in the main vase that is used during empowerments, which contains twenty-five different special substances. This water is so special that we are very careful not to spill it, as it contains great blessing. If you drink it, your poisonous afflictions will recede.

It's no use to have doubts or worry about such sacred substances. If you give rise to a lot of doubt about it, you won't receive the blessings. You may have a reason to worry and have doubts about eating different kinds of meat, because different meats can cause all sorts of disease, but mendrup is made from very sacred substances, so you don't need to worry about it.

It is said that if an ant eats just a tiny bit of this sacred medicine, it will be liberated from the three lower realms. If you carry this sacred medicine on your person, you will be protected from plagues and obstacles from negative forces. If you take some every day, you can be cured of many different types of illness. It also pacifies mental afflictions and conflicting emotions and gives rise to experiences and realization.

Most Westerners are not familiar with Dharma practice from childhood, so they often feel suspicious about things like this. In India and Nepal, often Westerners don't even want to drink the blessed water from the vase during an empowerment; they think the water is not pure, so they won't drink it and instead just touch their lips to it and then put it on their head. But as long as one has doubts about these things, it will be difficult to accomplish anything in the Dharma.

Mingyur Dorje

THE NAMCHÖ CYCLE that we practice in the Palyul tradition is a treasure revelation of Terchen Mingyur Dorje's, so I'd like to relate some of his history.

Mingyur Dorje had about five hundred different lifetimes, manifesting in each of the six realms to benefit innumerable beings. He especially manifested in the hells and liberated many of the beings there. He said that he didn't experience any of the sufferings in hell and that due to his power and realization, he emptied out many of the hells. Due to their strong karma, many of the hell beings could not be liberated by his usual methods. They got very angry with him and said, "We are suffering here, and you act like a hypocrite." Though he tried many methods, nothing worked, so he started chanting Avalokiteshvara's mantra, *Om mani padma hum,* to a very beautiful tune and blew sand on the hell fires to extinguish them. In this way, he liberated countless hell beings. He also took many births in the animal realm, as tiny insects and as larger animals like birds, goats, and so forth, and he liberated innumerable animals by teaching them in a manner that conformed to their species.

Mingyur Dorje was born in India many times. Before Buddha Shakyamuni appeared in this world, he was born as an Indian prince who used to collect jewels from the ocean. Being a prince, he used to carry a net with clothes on his back, which was called a *jaga,* so they called him Jagapa. For a long time he wandered around in search of a master named Apara but was unable to find him. Master Apara, however, knew that the prince was looking for him, so he waited for him at a certain place, but when Prince Jagapa arrived, he didn't recognize Apara and actually asked him if he knew where Apara could be found. At that moment, Apara flew up to a rock, where he left his footprints, and remained there. Jagapa became very devoted, relied on him as his teacher, and started receiving teachings. After practicing the teachings he was given, Jagapa attained accomplishment and gathered many students, among whom were three who became mahasiddhas with great miraculous power.

During the time of Buddha Shakyamuni, Mingyur Dorje was born as the Buddha's half brother Ananda. He acted as the Buddha's attendant and a custodian of the Buddha's teachings, guarding the doctrine for a long time. Later, when Padmasambhava went to Tibet, Mingyur Dorje was born both as the great translator Vairotsana and as a yogi called Shubu Palgyi Senge, who translated many Sanskrit teachings into Tibetan, spread the Secret Mantrayana teachings in Tibet, and accomplished everything that Padmasambhava told him to do.

Later he took birth in Tibet at a place called Ngam, where he started giving teachings when he was three or four years old. His parents, however, wondered what kind of ghost language he was speaking and didn't revere him at all. When he was about eleven years old, he met Karma Chakme Rinpoche, who recognized that he was a special reincarnation and invited him to stay at his place. At Chakme Rinpoche's place, he stayed with his tutor for a long time, which resulted in a bit of obscuration. So Chakme Rinpoche gave him a lot of purification nectar to cure the obscuration, and later Mingyur Dorje began to have many pure visions of various deities, which is how the Namchö teachings were gradually revealed. When Chakme Rinpoche started teaching him the different scripts, Mingyur Dorje told him, "I know all those scripts." He then wrote down the scripts of many different countries and asked Chakme Rinpoche, "Do you know these?" But Chakme Rinpoche had to admit that he didn't. Though Chakme Rinpoche was Mingyur Dorje's guru, when Mingyur Dorje started revealing the Namchö cycle, Chakme Rinpoche then took Mingyur Dorje as his master.

When Mingyur Dorje was still quite young, a buddha was about to pass into nirvana in another buddha field, so Mingyur Dorje had to go there as a representative and to attain perfect enlightenment. Because of this, he only lived in this world for about nineteen years.

The Namchö cycle is the exact Dharma teaching appropriate for this time. It is very condensed and profound and has a great deal of blessings. The entire cycle was directly transmitted from Avalokiteshvara to Mingyur Dorje. The cycle then passed from Chakme Rinpoche to Rigdzin Kunzang Sherab. From Rigdzin Kunzang Sherab down to the present day, the Palyul lineage Namchö teachings were transmitted from master to disciple, and each of these masters was very special and attained accomplishment. All of the vajra masters who practiced this cycle had special signs when passing away and didn't die in an ordinary manner.

The followers of the Namchö teachings spread all over eastern Tibet and established thousands of monasteries. When Kunzang Sherab was alive, he had students all over eastern Tibet, and later when he moved to the retreat place called Dhako, he had tens of thousands of followers. It is said that these followers then spread and established about a thousand branch monasteries, and each of those monasteries had many special lamas and tulkus who were true bodhisattvas. Nowadays, it's customary to write detailed biographies of such masters, but at that time such things weren't done. Each lama would just do their practice, accomplish the teachings, gather disciples, and lead them on the path to liberation. Instead of telling stories about themselves, they spent their entire life concentrating on practice.

Everything is included and complete in this cycle, from the preliminaries up to the trekchö and thögal practices of the Great Perfection. These teachings have inconceivable blessings, and if you have faith and devotion and practice correctly, even if you don't receive many signs, at least you won't be afraid at the time of death.